AMITY
UNIVERSITY PRESS

My Vibrant Planet

Environmental Studies Series

Mohina Dar • Gitanjali Khanduri

Best Seller
Reference Book

Name ______________________

Class ______________ Section ______________

School ______________________

PREFACE

The study of Social Science, is at the best of times, both comprehensive and profound and of utmost importance in the holistic development of the child.

The present series for young minds of classes 4 and 5 is an attempt towards helping the child to empathise with the environment and move towards constructive learning.

The book is strictly in accordance with the new curriculum prescribed by NCERT. The book is child friendly, providing the young reader opportunities to explore, question, discuss and do group work in order to understand the spirit of the lesson. Along with these, there are several interesting hands-on-activities, short stories, puzzles, jumbles, illustrations, poems and experiments.

An attempt has been made to accommodate the vast diversity of people and communities of the country. We, as adults, need to ensure that our future citizens are not only aware of multi-facetedness of our country, but will also learn to appreciate their value and respect these differences.

Great care has been taken to keep the text lively, colourful and meaningful, to make learning a pleasurable experience. The narratives and examples are taken from contemporary situations so that the child can easily relate to them. The stories are from everyday life and the characters are meant to inspire and motivate the child to strive towards a healthier and happier community living.

It goes without saying that evaluation remains a continuous process of the teaching-learning methodology. The child's analysis and understanding of the lesson is evaluated through regular question answer method as well as objective exercises, games and puzzles.

The authors believe that the teacher remains the most important link between the child and the written word and as such what the child grows up to be, largely rests on the able shoulders of the teacher. Hence, teachers should feel free to use the book as one of the aids in the other teaching-learning methods and improvise as and when required.

The authors wish to extend their grateful thanks to Mr. R. R. Aiyar and the able team at AUP. Special thanks also goes to our families who endured tough times and shared our joys and disappointments with equal fervour.

Feedback and suggestions from the readers regarding any aspect of the book are always welcome.

Mohina Dar • Gitanjali Khanduri

Contents

Unit 1: Families On The Move

Chapter 1

The Ever Changing Family

Note To The Teacher

Most of us take family life for granted. But, the family system is undergoing change. This chapter explains how family life is affected by the changes in society. It also helps develop better understanding of our own and other people's families.

Learning Points

- Definition of a family.
- Importance of a family.
- Transition from extended (joint) families to nuclear families.
- Modern form of families.

GLOSSARY Social animal, joint family, nuclear family, selfish genes, adoptive, foster, single parent family.

Humans are social animals, which means that people do not like to live alone. People all over the world have always lived in groups. But, the type of group they live in, depends on factors such as culture, religions, etc. Equally important are the smaller social groups like our friends, neighbours, etc.

And above all, is the family!

People living in the same region belong to the same regional group.

Note To The Teacher On the political map of India help students identify and mark Kashmir and Karnataka.

A Typical Indian Family

So, What Is A Family?

A family is a group of people tracing their origin from a common ancestor. Family gives us a sense of who we are and where we are from. Family is, therefore, a source of great happiness.

Why Have A Family?

Family life provides the support needed for survival. It also provides security, love and comfort.

Our life would be very tough indeed if we had no families.

Common Physical Traits

Most members of a family will carry with them certain common physical features and it is these traits which enable others to recognise a group of people belonging to one family.

Now list out at least two habits that you share with another member of your extended family:

1. ____________________

2. ____________________

Read the story in the box to understand this better.

We Are Alike

This is the true story of Hemanta, an 11 year old boy from the village of Rasulpur, who was lost and then got reunited with his family.

"It was the year 2006. The harvesting season had just got over and we were all planning to go to the annual Mahashivya fair, in the village nearby. On the day of the fair, my brothers and I woke up early and excitedly got dressed. Baba, amma and we had our breakfast of chappatis, vegetables and tea and then we left for the fair.

It looked as if people from all corners were thronging the fair. Suddenly, the clouds burst and there was a tremendous downpour.

Everyone began running helter-skelter. In the ensuing chaos, I got separated from my family. Some hours later when it began drizzling, some rescuers found me hiding in the hole of a tree. One of them, I don't remember who immediately on seeing me asked, “Aren't you Shanoo Devi's son?” “Yes”, I replied weakly. Within an hour I was reunited with my family.

“Do you know how this miracle happened? You see, my amma and I share an uncanny resemblance. We both have arched eyebrows and a broad forehead. This physical similarity saved me that day.”

Now answer the following questions.

Your one special physical feature.	Who is it similar to?	Some features of yours, unlike any other in the family.
______________	______________	______________

There are also some physical features and habits that may be similar to members of our extended family. These physical features and habits are transferred to the next generation by units of heredity called genes.

Family Structure From Joint Family To Nuclear

The structure of the family has varied greatly throughout history in different societies around the world.

Joint Family System

You have already learnt in your earlier class about extended families. When grandparents, children and grandchildren all live together it is called **a joint family system**.

The head of the family is usually the senior most family member like a grandfather or grandmother.

Living in a joint family has many advantages over a nuclear family. In a joint family, the weak can depend on the strong and many tasks like childcare can be shared. Most importantly, moral values, skills and knowledge can be passed down from one generation to another.

Distant relatives sometimes are not so distant after all.

Nuclear Family

A family where only the mother, father and their children live together is called a **nuclear family**.

Nuclear means the centre point and a nuclear family is the centre point of a larger group of relatives who live elsewhere.

Nuclear families generally come up when people move out, especially from their hometown to other places in search of work. In such a situation, maintaining ties with members of the extended family becomes a bit difficult.

A nuclear family

Now let us make a family tree for Rahul. Study the family tree given below and make a similar family tree of your friend.

HINT : Talk to your friend's mother and find out more about the family members.

Activity

List out at least two more reasons why nuclear families are becoming more common.

1. ______________________________

2. ______________________________

Hint: Compare your house to that of your grandparents'.

The Amazing Selfish Genes

Why do we feel a close bond with family members, even though we sometimes get angry and have fights with them? One important reason is that we share many genes in common. If we cooperate and take care of each other, we help our genes to survive. This is called the **selfish gene theory**.

Isn't this amazing?

All children share one half of their genes with one of their parents and the remaining with their grandparents, brothers, sisters, uncles, aunts and cousins.
These genetic links tell us the reason behind the closeness we share with our relatives and the concern we have for them.

Times Are Changing

Families today are taking many different forms.
Let's see this through a pictorial representation.

Adoptive Families

My parents adopted me when I was 3 months old. They are the most loving and caring parents and I am very proud of them.
I hope they are proud of me too.

Foster Families

When my parents died in an accident, my father's best friend took care of me and today I live happily with my foster brother, sister and parents. I remember my real parents too, but my new parents never let me be upset for long.

Single Parent Families

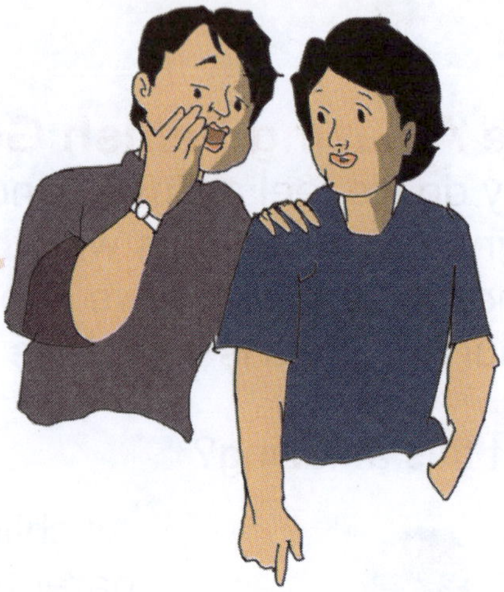

When our mother died our father felt lonely and lost. But, now after two years things are more stable. We all help and take care of each other. In fact, sometimes we cook food for our dad and sometimes he cooks for us.

Family Values

While living in a nuclear family, we must remember to give due respect and care to all members of the extended family. We must share work according to our age and ability. We must care for each other and provide support to those in need.

Let's wind up with a tricky family puzzle.

Who am I?

1. I am your father's sister's daughter.
   I am your ______________________________________

2. Your maternal grandfather is the only male member in the family from our generation. I am his first cousin.
   You can call me ______________________________________

3. I am your mother's, mother's aunt.
   So, you can consider me your ______________________________________

Fascinating Facts

- Tribals and nomads all over the world live in large communities as one family and share their joys and sorrows with each other.
- In Israel, childcare is usually shared, and a few adults look after all the children of a village.

Points to Remember

1. Humans live in groups. The most important group is the family.
2. Most family members share some common physical traits.
3. When many members of a family live together, it is called a joint family.
4. When only parents and their children live together, it is called a nuclear family.
5. Different types of families are becoming more common, for example, adoptive or single parent families.

Remember

All family members must do some careful juggling and share the work. You cannot afford to think only about yourself and ignore the wishes of the other family members.

A happy family simply means a family that works together and cares about each other.

Exercises

1. Answer the following questions.

   (a) Why are humans known as social animals?

   (b) What is a regional group?

   (c) What is a family? Why is a family important?

(d) What helped the rescuers in tracing Hemanta's family when he got separated from them?

(e) What is the advantage of a joint family?

(f) What are some of the values that we need to take care of while living in a nuclear family?

(g) Explain the reason for the closeness and concern we feel towards our family members and relatives.

2. Fill in the blanks.

(a) Humans are known as ....

(b) A family provides ...., ... and ....

(c) We may be having certain features which we share with a number of our ....

(d) All children share .... of their genes with of their parents.

(e) .... and .... live in large communities as one family.

Fun Time

1. Make a family tree on a chart paper — remember to complete it according to your own paternal family. Start with great grandfather weds great grandmother.

2. Now let's begin another interesting activity. You are familiar with a family tree. Make a family tree of the women from your mother's side of the family. (Let's see how far you can get!)

Unit 1: Families On The Move

Chapter 2

Human Migration

Note To The Teacher

This lesson will help students understand key concepts of human migration through different migratory patterns. It will help students gain information about communities on the move. Teachers to explain to the students that this lesson will focus on the movements of large groups of people from one place to another and explain the reasons for their movement.

Learning Points

- What is migration?
- Why do people migrate?
- Different types of migrations.
- Problems faced by migratory communities.

GLOSSARY Communities, public services, migration, nomads, casual-migrant workers.

Systematic or regular movement of a community of or some families from one region to another is called **migration**. Migration can take place from one nearby place to another or over very long distances, like another state or country. This movement of people is called **human migration**. For example, Rani and her family will be moving from Chennai to Bhopal as Rani's father has got a new job. They are migrating to Bhopal.

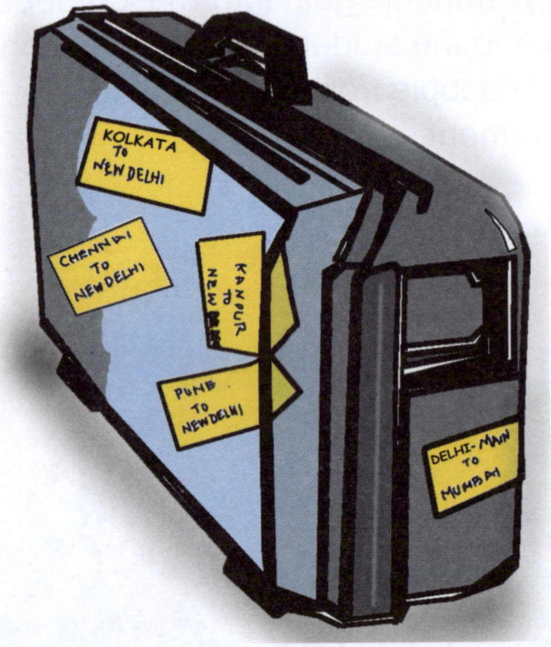

Do You Know?

Today, every third person in India is a city dweller.

Activity

On the political map of India mark Chennai and Bhopal. With the help of a scales join the two cities.

Migration is of different types.

In this chapter we will discuss three types of migration.

Migration

- **From village to city**
- **Nomads**
- **Transfer/posting**

Let's study them in detail

From Villages To Cities

Cities attract people from the villages because they seem to promise a more prosperous life.

People in villages work very hard. But sometimes a natural disaster might strike the village or people may not be able to find suitable jobs.

They, therefore, are eager to move to towns and cities in search of jobs or better prospects. And sometimes there are natural causes of migrations too, for example, a change in climate, floods or severe shortage of water. But moving to a town is not always a good solution as they may not get the job they dreamt of or a place to live. They may not be able to send their children to school and there could be many other unexpected problems.

But travelling to another place for a few days is not migration.

Activity

With so much migration to cities there must be heavy pressure on public services. With the help of your teacher list out some common problems.

Hint: You can include lack of water as one of the problems.

....

....

....

....

....

Now, read this true story about Meena who lived happily in the village with her parents and four siblings till disaster struck.

Meena's Story

One day, the rains came down very heavily. It continued to pour for the next five days. Everything in the village got washed away. My parents and we five siblings took **shelter** on a tree until we were finally rescued by the army. At the **relief camp**, everyone said that the river goddess was angry. I wondered what we had done to face her wrath.

After some days when things were little better, my father went to our house to check.

There was nothing left. Disheartened, my parents decided to migrate to the city in search of a job.

That was 3 years ago. I am now 15 years old. My mother and I work as domestic help in the nearby apartments, while my father runs a tea stall.

The rains changed our lives forever.

Would you call the movement by Meena's family a transfer or a forced migration? Why?

....

....

....

Teacher To Discuss

How is a temporary / short term job different from a permanent job?

Nomads

Not all people migrate from one place to another to find jobs or due to some emergencies. There are many communities in the world which move from one place to place, according to the seasons, in search of food, water and grazing land. They are known as **nomads**.

Nomads do not live at one place all the time. They constantly move taking their belongings with them. So, they do not build permanent homes. They live in tents and caravans.

Nomads mainly travel to

- find work for themselves
- find food and water for their herds of animals.

Do You Know?

Many people take up a job for a short period of time in the cities. They are called **casual migrant workers.**

It is interesting to note that nomads generally travel with their animals. They always have dogs with them too. Can you say why?

Transfer/Posting

Fascinating Facts

Nomadic communities in India comprise 7% of the country's population. Some of them do farming, while others are engaged in non-farming activities. Here's a list of some of the nomads in India - **Gujjars** of **Jammu and Kashmir**, **Gaddis** of **Himachal Pradesh**, **Dhangars** of **Maharashtra**, etc.

Note To The Teacher With the help of a political map of India, help children identify the previously mentioned states.

Not all people move because of a problem. Sometimes the adults in the family get transferred / posted to another place. In such a situation, the family also has to move to a new place.

There can be other reasons too for such migrations:

- one of the parents gets a new job in another town
- either parent starts a new business
- sometimes people shift to be close to old grandparents or other relatives

To be conducted by teachers

Pass one or more index cards to each student and ask them to write down the name of the state where they hail from. As each card represents one state some students may need multiple (two or more) cards. Later the cards can be put on the class board and students can find out the maximum number of classmates belonging from one state.

Do You Know?

People consistently move to better regions. Let's take the example of a nomadic community of Rajasthan. The **Raikas** of **Rajasthan** stay in their villages in the monsoon seasons as there is enough water available in the village. But by October when there is shortage of water, they move to another place in search of pasture and water.

Points to Remember

1. Constant movement of people from one place to another is called migration.
2. There are different types of migrations.
3. Some people move in search of jobs from villages to cities.
4. Some communities do not have a permanent place to stay and move about according to the seasons and their needs. They are called nomads.

Exercises

1. **Answer the following questions.**

   (a) Explain the word migration.

   (b) Why do people migrate from villages to cities?

   (c) Make a list of different types of migrations.

   (d) Why do nomads migrate? What kind of homes do they live in?

   (e) Why do you think the Raika community of Rajasthan is different from other nomadic communities?

2. **Give one word answers for the following.**

   (a) Movement of people from one region to another. ....

   (b) People who work in cities for a short period of time. ....

(c) People who live in tents and caravans and do not have a permanent home. ....

(d) The nomadic community in Rajasthan who live during monsoons in their own village. ....

(e) Migrations also happens when parents set up a new business. ....

3. Unjumble the following words to get the correct answer.

(a) IRATGMNOI

(b) SMNDOA

(c) IVRELTAE

4. Match the following Indian nomadic communities with the states they belong to

Column A	**Column B**
(a) Raikas	Maharashtra
(b) Dhangars	Jammu & Kashmir
(c) Gaddis	Rajasthan
(d) Gujjars	Himachal Pradesh

5. Group activity

To be done with the help of teachers by small groups or with the whole class. Ask students to prepare a collage of families on the move.

Fun Time

With the help of an adult, find two people in your neighbourhood who have shifted from the place of their origin to your town. Interview them. They can be your domestic help, the neighbourhood cobbler or a neighbourhood family.

Hints: You can ask questions like why did this person leave his own town? Did he/she move alone or with the family? What difficulties they faced?

Chapter 3

Likes And Dislikes

Note To The Teacher

This lesson will help students understand that a community comprises people from different parts of the country with different taste in food habits, dressing styles, etc. Teachers should aim to sensitize of students about the cultural likes and dislikes of their classmates to facilitate a healthier environment in the class.

Learning Points

- Different set of habits depend upon climate and country.
- Variations in food habits.
- Different styles of dresses.
- Herbal medicines.

GLOSSARY Traditions, customs, melting pot, climate, export, alternative medicines.

People in different parts of the world have their own ways of doing things. These are called traditions and customs.

Traditions and customs affect how people behave, it also influences what they eat, what they wear and how they celebrate important occasions in their lives.

When a group or community shares similar customs relating to religion, language, clothes, foods, sports, entertainment, etc., they are said to have similar cultural traits.

Mary belongs to America. She has been brought up in a Western culture. They eat their food with a knife and fork from a plate.

Aileen is from China. She has been brought up in the Chinese culture, food is eaten with chopsticks.

Raghav and Ritika are from India. Generally, they eat food without using forks, spoons or knives, greet people by putting their hands together and bowing their heads. They also offer sweets during festivals.

Make a chart and write different forms of greetings in as many Indian languages as possible.

Merging of cultures

The people's likes and dislikes is affected a great deal by their cultural background. You have probably learnt some of your own values by growing up in a particular culture.

As people have migrated around the world, they have taken their own culture with them too. This multicultural mix is sometimes called the melting pot.

Wedding between two families of different religions, traditions and rituals results in the merging of two different families and cultures.

In this chapter, we will discuss two aspects of differences amongst people:

(a) eating habits

(b) dressing style.

Different People, Different Cuisines

One area of great variation is the food patterns of the people.

Food habits are based on the kind of crops grown in the region. Climate too affects food habits. The most popular food grains in our country are rice and wheat. Wheat is grown in plenty in the northern Indian states. Rice is an Important part of the diet of the people in eastern and southern parts of India.

Do You Know?

In classical dance, Bharatanatyam, every movement has a meaning. But you can't understand it if you haven't watched the dance carefully or learnt something about it.

Cereals like wheat, rice, lentils, ragi, pulses (dal) are popular in all parts of the country.

Look at the chart below to understand this better.

State	Food
Punjab	Chapatti, sarson ka saag
Kerala	Rice and fish with lots of coconut
Rajasthan	Jowar, bajra, corn
West Bengal	Rice, daal, fish and sweets

Spicy India

In the midst of all these differences, there is one common feature. All Indians love to eat a variety of spices in different forms. India is the largest producer of spices in the world. It supplies spices to different parts of the world. Sending products to another country and selling them there to earn money is called export.

Fascinating Facts

An ear of **wheat** is made up of at least 40-60 grains. Wheat is harvested after its grains turn golden yellow.

More than 40% of the world's rice is produced in Asia. Therefore, most Asians love to eat rice.

Can you name some commonly used spices in your home?

Hint: Take help from your mother.

Fruits

We all love eating different fruits. Though we buy different fruits from market, some of them are easily available in plenty in different parts of the country.

Let's see some popular fruits in India and where they come from.

Places	Fruits
Nagpur	Oranges
Assam, Goa	Pineapples
Himachal Pradesh, Jammu & Kashmir	Apples

Fascinating Facts

Most of us eat green or red (or sometimes both) chillies in food that is cooked at home. Some people even eat them raw. Kishan Chandra Joshi of the state of Uttar Pradesh grew a chilli plant that is the highest in the world, 6.6 metres!

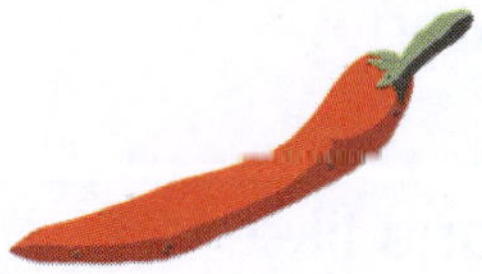

In a typical vegetarian home in Punjab, what do you think a day's menu would be? Find out and write:

(a) Breakfast ....

(b) Lunch..............................

(c) Dinner..............................

Here are some questions for you.

First ask your friend what his/her favourite traditional food item is?

Find out which state is famous for that food? ....

Now, tell what is your favourite food item and which state is famous for it?..

Teacher To Organise

A traditional food party in the class.
Each student can bring one food item typical of their state. Let the other students find out what it is called.
Eat and enjoy!

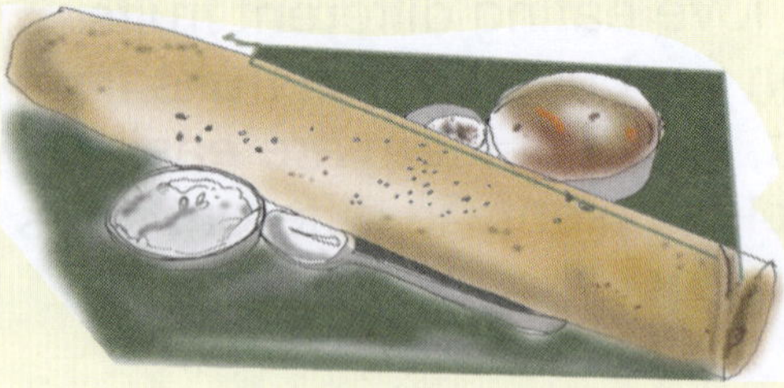

Read the following story to understand how difficult it can sometimes be to adjust to different eating habits.

Ma, I am hungry

...Aton was excited. He was coming to Ahmedabad as part of student exchange programme from Nagaland. As the landscape changed from lush green to the hot and dry landscape of Gujarat, Aton also felt a little nervous. He was received at the railway station by Mrs. and Mr. Patel who would be his host for the next seven days that he would be there. Mr. Patel was also the principal of the school Aton would be attending. Mrs. Patel hugged Aton and welcomed him. At home, a mouth watering lunch awaited him. Rice was the first dish Aton took on his plate. It reminded him of home. It was followed by dal and vegetables. Aton found each dish tasting a little sugary or sweet. Mrs. Patel explained that in Gujarat all dishes have a little sugar added to them. After a few days, however, Aton couldn't relish the food any longer.

Moreover, Mrs. and Mr. Patel were vegetarians like most other Gujaratis whereas Aton, like others from Nagaland, was a non-vegetarian. At the end of the week, it was time for Aton to return. He had enjoyed his stay. But he was missing home.

As Kohima approached Aton could see the greenery from the window of the plane he had boarded from Kolkata. It reminded him of home, hot food, specially rice and soup. The first thing Aton told his mother after hugging her was "Ma, I am hungry. Give me some food please."

Why do you think Aton asked his mother for food?

Did Mrs. Patel not give him food to eat? Have a class discussion on this.

Dressing Up India

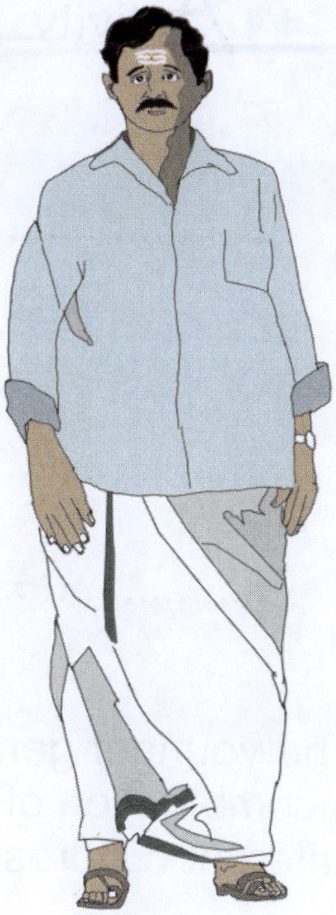

People from different parts of the country look different not only due to their features, but also because of clothes and jewellery they wear.

The type of clothes people wear often depends on the climate and place where they live. Some places in India are extremely hot in summers and some places are extremely cold in winters. Some live near the sea, in coastal areas. Anitha, for example, is from Cochin in Kerala. Her father wears a shirt with a lungi (called Mundu) when he is relaxing at home.

But Carole's parents, who are from Goa, prefer to wear Bermuda shorts and T-shirts at home.

Most Indian women wear sarees. The saree is a 3000 years old garment. Though, saree is worn in most parts of the country, the style of wearing the saree depends on different states.

Find out how the women in Bengal traditionally tie their saree.

Activity

Most Indian states have their special weave of sarees. For example, Maheshwari saree belongs to Madhya Pradesh. Find out the names of six other types of sarees. List them here.

....

....

....

....

The younger generation, however, wears a combination of clothes belonging to different cultures.

If you are a girl, your cupboard may be full of skirts, shorts, lehengas for special occasions and probably one or two salwar kameez or churidars.

And, if you are a boy you probably have an almirah full of jeans, shorts, pants and even a suit or churidar kurta for special occasions.

Do You Know?

There are many traditional medicines hundreds of years old that are still very popular. Though, most people approach an allopathic doctor when they are unwell, many prefer alternative medicines like herbal medicines, homeopathic treatment or ayurveda. Some people practice yoga to stay fit and recover from illness.

Note To The Teacher

Discuss a little more about homeopathic and ayurvedic medicines.

Traditional way of thinking help people to feel that they belong to a special and unique group. People who migrate from one place to another, like to maintain links with their original culture. They do this by forming organizations and meeting each other regularly, e.g. there are many Indian organizations in foreign countries, where people of Indian origin meet up with each other on special occasions.

Do you know of any such organisation?

Points to Remember

1. People in different parts of the country have their own way of doing things.
2. Migration of people to different parts of the world has led to the world becoming a "melting pot."
3. Climate plays a very important role in deciding the food and dress habits of people.
4. Alternative medicines like ayurveda and herbal medicines are very popular with many people.

Exercises

1. Answer the following questions.
   (a) Name the two most popular food grains consumed in India.
   (b) When is it said that people have similar cultural traits? What does it mean.
   (c) What is a melting pot?
   (d) Define export.
   (e) What does the dressing style of people depend on?

2. Fill in the blanks.

(a) In Chinese culture food is eaten with ____________________ .

(b) An ear of wheat is made up of ____________________ grains.

(c) Himachal Pradesh is famous for this fruit ____________________.

(d) The traditional dress of men in Kerala is the shirt and lungi. It is called ______________.

(e) Maheshwari saree is produced in the state of ______________.

(f) Alternative medicines include ______________, ______________ and ______________.

3. Tick the correct answer.

(a) Rice is mainly eaten by people of

(i) Northern India

(ii) Eastern India

(b) Sending products to another country and selling them there is called

(i) Import

(ii) Export

(c) Oranges are grown in

(i) Nagpur

(ii) Kanpur

Fun Time

Circle the names of some of the dresses worn in India in the crossword puzzle.

C	H	U	R	I	D	A	R	P	S	M
X	Y	J	E	A	N	S	M	S	A	U
B	E	R	M	U	D	A	N	T	R	N
R	T	S	K	I	R	T	O	C	E	D
L	E	H	E	N	G	A	S	F	E	U
S	A	L	W	A	R	U	O	V	X	C
U	K	A	M	E	E	Z	C	M	P	O

Unit 2: Work and Play

Chapter 4

Dignity Of Labour

Note To The Teacher

This lesson aims to discuss the sensitive topic of menial workers. Teachers to discuss the importance of showing respect for all kinds of work and learning to be self-dependant.

Learning Points

- Importance of helpers.
- What would happen if some helpers stopped working?
- All occupations deserve same respect and dignity.
- Importance of Mahatma Gandhi in bringing equality amongst people.
- Who are human scavengers?

GLOSSARY

Occupations, dignity, kachrawali, inequality, self-dependant, manual scavengers, rehabilitation, beautician.

In Delhi, Vineeta's mother was getting very upset. The house was untidy. Even the utensils had not been washed. Everything was in a big mess. She had no choice, but to leave the house untidy. She had to reach her office on time. While travelling in the bus to office, she suddenly realized what a great help Taposhi, the domestic help, was. The house was so spic and span all because of Taposhi. However, today she had not come at her usual time.

As Vineeta's mother looked up from her thoughts she saw the bus driver and the conductor. She thought to herself, what if they did not come on duty too. What would happen then? While getting down from the bus she remembered to thank them and wish them a good day.

Vineeta's mother is not alone. Similar problems are faced by many people in different places.

In Chennai, Mrs. Kumar is wondering why the big dustbins in the corridors are not being cleaned.

Mrs. Kumar

In Kolkata, Mr. Bhattacharya and his family feel the colony has become unsafe as the security guard has gone to his village on leave.

Mr. Bhattacharaya

In Lucknow, Robin and John felt sick going to the school toilet today. It was smelling and the floor was wet and dirty. The reason was that the cleaner did not come to work.

Robin and John

These are very, real situations. They can happen anywhere. And, if they happen too often, can you imagine what our city and homes would look like?

Perhaps, they would become:

unclean

unhygienic

messy

unsafe

uncomfortable

unhappy

Think about it!!

Unclean environment leads to:

1. Dirty surroundings and impure air and water.
2. Bad smell and unpleasant neighbourhood.
3. More flies, mosquitoes and other dangerous insects.
4. Spread of infections and diseases.

So, isn't it extremely important to respect the work people do to keep our environment clean and healthy?

Dignity Of Labour

Garbage picker

People are engaged in different occupations. All occupations are equally important. Some may be engaged in office jobs, which require special skills and training. Some may require a great deal of travelling.

But, if there is no one to help us clean our homes and neighbourhood, give us the morning newspaper, operate lights in the apartments or clean the neighbourhood sewage drain pipes, would we be able to lead normal lives?

Remember

People who sweep the roads, clean the sewage lines or repair shoes are as important in our lives as engineers, doctors or office workers. People engaged in different occupations should be addressed respectfully. Never look down on the occupations of others.

"I Also Deserve Dignity"

Deepa Kumari is a garbage collector in a colony. She wakes up at 4:00 in the morning and reports for duty by 6:30 a.m. She first sweeps the roads and then moves from house to house picking up the garbage. She feels sad and humiliated when some children call her a kachrawali.

She likes it when children address her as didi. It brings a smile on her face and gives her the dignity she deserves.

Deepa Kumari

This Is What She Has To Say

"Some residents are very considerate. They divide the garbage into two packs. The kitchen waste in one and the rest in the other. My hands do not get dirty on picking up such garbage. But, some people just dump all the garbage in the dustbin and I have to pick things by hand and put them in my big cart. Yesterday, some broken glass had been thrown and I cut my hand and it began to bleed. My friend tore a portion of her dupatta and tied my hand. I wish people were more considerate towards us."

How is garbage disposed off in your home?

____

____

What would happen in the colony if Deepa Kumari does not report to work? Tick on yes or no.

(1) Would the roads be clean? Yes / No

(2) Would the garbage give off bad smell? Yes / No

(3) Would you like it, if sudden guests arrive at your home in such a situation? Yes / No

You too can help Deepa Kumari in maintaining cleanliness in your colony. Answer these questions in yes or no.

(1) Can you organise volunteers to sweep the roads if Deepa Kumari is on leave? Yes / No

(2) Can you request your neighbours to be careful while disposing off waste? Yes / No

(3) Can you encourage other children in the colony to address the cleaners and scavengers with respect? Yes / No

Who Cares?

Has anyone ever tried to make a difference in the lives of these people? The answer is, yes. In our country, there have been great leaders who have specially tried to help the downtrodden. Many people are making similar efforts even today.

Gandhi ji

Mahatma Gandhi, the father of our nation, was one of them. He believed that everyone is equal. He also believed that everyone should take pride in doing their own work. He said that this was the only way everyone would become equal. He always led by example. He did everything that he asked others to do.

Read On:

Gandhiji wanted people to respect others for the work they did. He also felt that people would appreciate them only if they had to do the same work themselves. So, he made sure that in his ashram everyone did all the work including, cleaning the toilets themselves. Many people did not like this. Some got so angry that they left the ashram. Even Gandhiji's wife, Kasturba, did not like doing this work on her own at first. But slowly, everyone started doing the menial jobs on their own. It was then that they realised that one does not lose dignity by doing menial work. They become self-dependent.

The sad truth, however, is that people like Gandhiji alone cannot change society. Even today, there are lakhs of people who are looked down upon due to their occupation. Manual scavengers are one of them. They collect garbage from dustbins and from outside.

The government wants to improve the working condition of manual scavengers very soon. For that purpose, it has started providing different kind of training to them with the use of new equipments. This is called Rehabilitation.

Reena and Mayank

Remember

Improving the working conditions in each occupation is a way of giving dignity to the workers.

Beautician

Reena and Mayank have been given a school project to find out more about manual scavengers. Why don't you team up with a friend and prepare your own report? The activity given below will help you.

Activity

Talk to any of the staff members who mop and clean the floors in your school. You can ask them the following questions:

1. Since when are they working in the school?

   ....

2. What problems do they face?

   ....

3. In what ways can we help?

   ....

Points to Remember

1. People are engaged in different occupations.
2. Those who provide general services are called helpers.
3. Many people tend to look down on some occupations.
4. Mahatma Gandhi, the father of our nation, believed that all people and all occupations are equal.
5. Gandhiji also believed that everyone should do all their menial work themselves.

Exercises

1. Answer the following questions.

    (a) What would happen if there was no one to help us complete our household work?

    (b) How do good residents behave with Deepa Kumari?

    (c) What do you understand by dignity of labour?

    (d) Describe in brief Gandhiji's views on dignity of labour.

    (e) What measures has the government taken to improve the lives of menial workers?

2. Ratan Singh is an office peon. His motto in the office – "It is good to keep the office ______________ and ______________".
What work does Ratan Singh wants the office workers to do?
(Take the first letter from the group of words below, unjumble them and you'll get your words. Then write them in the above blanks.)

Nest Tap Action Egg

and

Elephant Night Achievement Crow Light

3. Here's a list of some helpers without whom we cannot live a comfortable life. They must be working near your residence too. Find out about their work and write them here. Speak briefly with them. Remember to be with an adult/guardian.

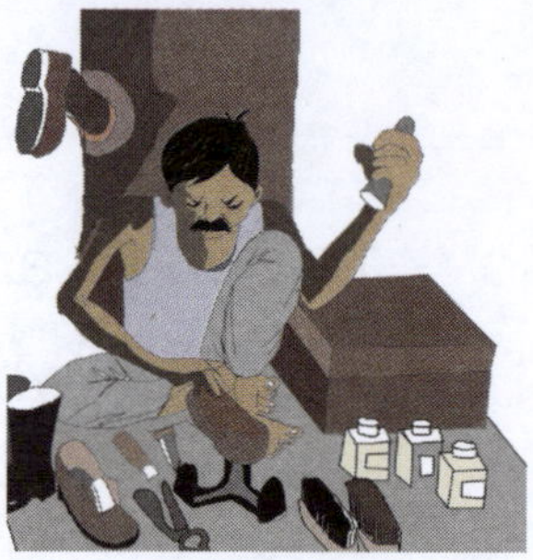

Cobbler

	Work
(a) Cobbler	(1) ....
(b) Tailor	(2) ....
(c) Garbage collector	(3) ....
(d) Bus cleaner	(4) ....
(e) Gardener	(5) ....
f. Vegetable shop cleaner boy	(6) ....

Rizvi, the school bus driver, is a little confused. A new bus route has been given to him. Help him go on the right path and drop all the children home.

Unit 2: Work and Play

Chapter 5

Team Sports

Note To The Teacher

This lesson aims to help students understand not only the difference between team and individual sports, but also the importance of team sports. Teachers should help students appreciate the traditional sports in India.

Learning Points

- What are team sports?
- Importance of team sports.
- Hockey, the national game of India.
- Importance of Arjuna Award.
- What are traditional sports?

GLOSSARY Guest of honour, Arjuna Award, national game, Olympics, martial arts, gymnastics.

Meera's grandparents, were at the bus stand to welcome her home. As the bus came to a halt, other parents and grandparents too crowded round the bus. Pride and happiness was visible on everyone's face. Just then, Meera got down with a huge shining trophy and everyone burst into claps and cheers.

Dadaji and Meera

She was followed by other girls and soon everyone was hugging them and shaking hands with them.

Are you wondering, what was happening at the bus stand?

Well, the girls' hockey team of Sunshine School had just returned after winning the state level interschool hockey championship!

Excitedly Meera said, "The medals were given by none other than the famous hockey player Gagan Ajit Singh. His speech has motivated me to perform even better."

"He's a brilliant hockey player. He has won the Arjuna Award and most importantly he has good **team spirit**", said another girl.

"Yes", added Dadaji. "He is a good role model."

Sports are an important part of our lives. We either play a game or watch others playing the game.

Sports, like cricket, which people enjoy watching are called **spectator sports**.

When one player competes against another, it is called an **individual sport**. For example tennis, golf, etc. Only one person wins in such sports.

That person becomes the champion. When a group of players compete against another group it's called **team sport**. For example, football, basketball, etc. A team sport cannot be played until each player feels part of the team. A team represents an institution, state or country.

Tennis player

Football match

Golfer

Do you play sports? If yes, then which one?

....

Is that an individual sport or a team sport?

....

Team Sports

A team sport has many advantages. It helps the players to grow and become more disciplined. Team sports also encourages leadership qualities, sportsmanship and cooperation, so that players learn to face healthy competition. Team sports build social skills and help people make new friends.

Hockey match

History Of Hockey

Hockey was introduced in India by Englishmen when they first arrived from England. Soon, Indians became world-class hockey players.

The Indian hockey team has won eight gold medals in the Olympic games. Hockey is the **National Game of India**.

The Star Of India

The world's greatest hockey player was Maj. Dhyan Chand. He represented India in the 3rd Olympic Games. It was said that he had magic in his hockey stick—The hockey ball, as it was, just stuck to his stick. His birthday, 29th August, is celebrated as the **National Sports Day.**

He was given many awards including the Padma Bhushan.

Maj. Dhyan Chand

Do You Know?

There is a statue of Maj. Dhyan Chand in Vienna, Austria.

Note To The Teacher

On the political map of the world show Austria.

Women too have not lagged behind in this sport. Players like Saba Anjum Karim and Gangotri Bhandari have brought laurels to the country.

Prem Maya Sonir is another player of high repute. She has taken part in many international hockey matches and has also been awarded the Arjuna Award by the government. She is now the coach of the Railway women's hockey team.

What Is The Arjuna Award?

The **Arjuna Award** is the prestigious award, which our government gives to sportspersons for outstanding sports performances. It is named after the great hero of *Mahabharata* — Arjuna. A bronze statue and a cash prize of ₹ 5 lakh is given to outstanding sports- persons. Just as hockey is India's national sport, other countries too have their national game. Here are a few:

Bangladesh	Canada	China	Germany	Japan	USA
Kabbadi	Ice Hockey	Ping-Pong	Football	Go	Baseball

Sports Awards in India

Arjuna Award: Arjuna Award recognises outstanding achievement in National sports.

Rajiv Gandhi Khel Ratna: Rajiv Gandhi Khel Ratna is India's highest honour given for achievement in sports.

Dhayan Chand Award: Dhayan Chand Award is named after legendary Indian hockey player Maj. Dhyan Chand and is given for lifetime achievement in sports.

Dronacharya Award: This award is presented by Government of India for excellence in sports coaching.

Girls Don't Play

"Grandmother, did you play any game? Were you a sportsperson too?" asked Meera. "I loved playing", replied grandmother. "But when I was young, girls were not encouraged to take part in sports. It was thought that girls were very delicate and would not be able to bear the harsh sun and tough life that sports involved. We only played some traditional games."

Traditional Sports

Sports that are being played in a country from ancient times are called **traditional sports**. Such sports activities are still as interesting to play and watch as they were hundreds of years ago.

Some traditional sports are still played in different parts of our country.

Let us take a look at them

The most popular traditional sport in India is **wrestling**. There are two contestants in wrestling. They hold each others waist and try to throw off each other, in such a way that their backs touch the ground. Wrestlers are not allowed to hit or punch each other.

Wrestling

Kabaddi is another popular traditional sport. It has two teams, which stand across a line on the ground. Breath control is very important in this sport. It can be played anywhere and has very simple rules.

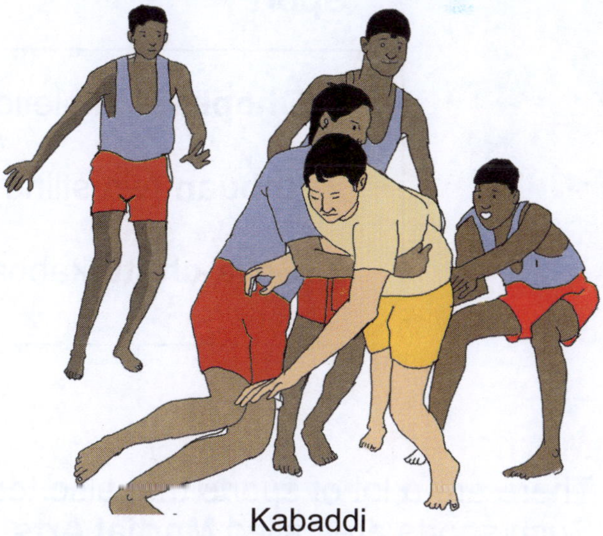

Kabaddi

Kite flying

A fun game for all children and adults is **kite flying**.

Traditionally, kites are flown after celebrating the festival of **Makar Sankranti** on 14th January.

Competitions in residential colonies also take place.

Yoga is another very popular activity, though it is not considered sport. Regular practice of yoga helps us become more disciplined, strong and calm.

Yoga

Which of these sports do you play?

....

Can you add more to the list of traditional sports?

....

Some traditional sports are only played in a particular part of the country. They have special names too. Have you heard of them?

Sport	State
1. **Dhopkhel** (athletic sport)	Assam
2. **Inbuan** (wrestling)	Mizoram
3. **Gella-chutt** (kabbadi)	Tripura

Martial Arts

There are a lot of sports that also teach self- defence. Such sports are called **Martial Arts.**

Martial Arts make us more confident and alert. Martial arts as a sport, have been practiced for thousands of years in India. Here are a few of them.

Kalaripayattu is very popular in **Kerala.** It is a mix of gymnastics which requires the use of wooden canes. It is very similar to **Karate**. Training for this sport begins at the age of 7.

Kalaripayattu

Another very popular martial art is **Mallakhamb** from the state of **Maharashtra.**

It is also known as **pole gymnastics.**

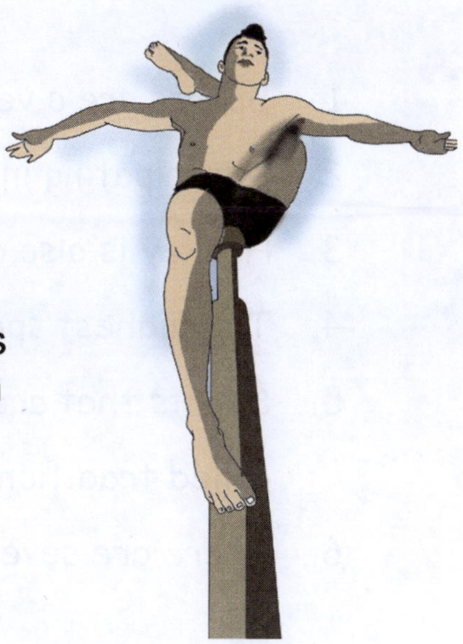

Archery with its use of bow and arrow is another popular sport. It is also an Olympic sport. Limba Ram is one of best archers from India.

Judo and **karate** are two extremely popular martial arts amongst children. Do you practice any one of them?

Mallakhamb

Archery

Activity

Rohan had been given a project activity. He had to visit the judo and karate centres in his neighbourhood. However, he has come down with chickenpox. Can you help him in completing the project activity by conducting it in your neighbourhood.

You will have to find out the following:

(a) The number of judo/karate training centres in your neighbourhood.

(b) How many students attend these classes?

(c) Do the students feel more confident after taking these classes? On a chart paper prepare a collage showing pictures of various kinds of martial arts sports. Later, the collages can be put up in your classroom.

Fascinating Facts

- Many of the sports played in present day, Olympics are the modern versions of the traditional games played in ancient India.
- Abhinav Bindra is the first Indian to win an individual gold medal in Olympics. He won it in the Beijing Olympics in 2008 for rifle shooting.

Abhinav Bindra

Points to Remember

1. Sports are a very important part of our lives.
2. Participating in team sports helps us face healthy competition.
3. Hockey is also a team sport.
4. The highest sports award in India is the The Khel Ratna Award.
5. Sports that are being played for thousands of years are called traditional sports.
6. There are several traditional sports that are still played in India.

Exercises

1. Answer the following questions.

(a) Why is playing team sports so important?

(b) Who introduced hockey in India? Why is hockey so important for India?

(c) What is the Arjuna Award?

(d) Why were girls not encouraged to play sports in the olden days?

(e) What are traditional sports? List out some popular ones played in India.

(f) How are martial arts important as a sport?

2. Differentiate between the following.

(a) Team sport and individual sport.

(b) Wrestling and kabbadi.

3. **Listed below are the names of some traditional sports. Rohan has jumbled up the letters in a hurry. Can you help him unscramble them?**

(a) BDIKBAA ....

(b) NAINUB ....

(c) NIGWERSLT ....

(d) TEKAAR ....

4. **The names of some sports have been given below. Can you identify what type of sport each is? Is it a team sport or an individual sport?**

	Team sport	Individual sport
Football		
Volleyball		
Gymnastics		
Chess		
Billiards		
Swimming		

5. **Given below are the names of some more sports. Circle the ones that come under the category of martial arts.**

Judo	Badminton	Baseball	Archery
Kalaripayattu	Throwball	Gymnastics	Mallakhamb
Karate	Cricket	Equestrian	Basketball

Fun Time

You need: Minimum two players, a dice and two different coloured counters. Begin at Start. Begin moving when you get 6 or 1 number on the dice. Follow the instructions.

Start	2	3	4	5	Bonus Go to 30	7	8	9	
10	11	12	13	14	15	16	17	18	
19	20	Miss a turn	22	23	24	25	26	27	
28	29	30	31	32	33	34	Bonus Go to 50	36	
37	38	39	40	41	42	Go to 13	44	45	
46	47	48	Bonus Go to 79	50	51	52	53	54	
55	56	57	58	59	60	61	Go to 22	63	
64	65	Miss a turn	67	68	69	70	71	72	
73	74	75	Bonus Go to 95	77	78	79	80	81	
82	83	84	85	86	87	88	89	90	
91	92	93	94	95	96	Go to 2	98	99	Winner

Unit 3: Wildlife: An Important Natural Resource

Chapter 6

Wildlife Protection

Note To The Teacher

Heartless killing of animals and cutting of trees in the forests have led to large scale destruction of wildlife and extinction of species. This section aims to help students understand the causes of extinction of animals and also, how wildlife can be protected. It is hoped that students will get sensitised towards wildlife protection.

Learning Points

- What are wildlife sanctuaries?
- There are many such sanctuaries in India.
- Animals need forests to live in.
- Reasons for vanishing forests.
- Efforts by government to save forests.

GLOSSARY Sanctuaries, hibernate, devastation, victims cycle, poaching, deforestation, habitation, vanmahotsava.

Where Are The Forests?

Rahul and his father were travelling by car to the Manas Wildlife Sanctuary in Assam. Their train had arrived late and it was already getting dark. The driver of the jeep was driving slowly and honking the car repeatedly. Rahul wanted to know why he was honking so much. The driver explained that wild elephants kept coming on the road at night. By honking, he was alerting them to stay away.

"Why do they come on the roads? Don't they like their forest?" said Rahul.

"What forest?" said the driver, "There's hardly any forests left."

He explained further that once upon a time the whole area was covered with thick forests, but people had cut away the trees and there was very little forest covering left. "That is why animals were forced to venture into the human habitation."

Isn't it a frightening thought? How would our earth look without forests? Imagine no tall trees, no clean running rivers and no wild animals. The earth would be very bare and impossible to live in. Forests are the natural home to wild animals.

There are many different kinds of animals in the wild.

1. **Terrestrial**
   For example, horses, camels etc.

Camel

2. **Aerial**
   For example, birds

Birds

3. **Arboreal**
   For example, monkey

Monkey

4. **Amphibian**
   For example, toad

Toad

5. **Aquatic**
   For example, fish

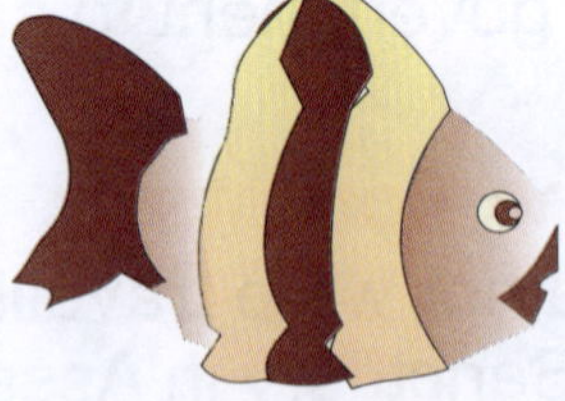

Fish

Due to the concern shown by individuals and various organisations, the government has set up some protected areas where killing of animals is not allowed. Cutting of trees is also prohibited in these areas.

India has a large variety of wild animals and birds. Many live in forests protected by the government. These are classified as:

- Wildlife sanctuaries
- National Parks
- Bird sanctuaries

There are about 150 wildlife sanctuaries in India.

Some of the animals found in these sanctuaries are not found anywhere in the world.

Tourists from all over the world visit our country to see them.

The chart below will tell you about some wild animals and where they are found.

Animals	State	National Parks/ Wildlife Sanctuary
Lions	Gujarat	Gir forest
Royal Bengal Tiger	West Bengal	Sunderbans Delta
One-horned Rhino	Assam	Kaziranga
Elephant	Kerala	Periyar
Tigers	Uttarakhand	Corbett

Find out and write the names of three more wildlife sanctuaries in India.

The reality is that animals too need forests. Here are some reasons.

1. Forests are full of food for animals. There are nuts, berries, leaves, insects and even other animals for them to eat.
2. Many creatures make their homes in trees.
3. Many animals can hibernate safely in winters.
4. They can hide from their enemies in forests.

Do You Know?

There were only 1411 tigers left in India today. In order to save them, **Project Tiger** was started in 1973 from the **Corbett National Park** in **Uttarakhand**.

Tiger

Note To The Teacher

Help students identify the wildlife sanctuaries on a political map of India.

However, due to growing population and surging need for forest products there has been a large scale **devastation** of animal habitats by humans. As a result, the animal population is declining. And, when the surviving animals do not find food for themselves, they attack domestic cattle and humans. In turn, they are killed by humans out of fear of their lives.

This is called a **vicious cycle of nature**.

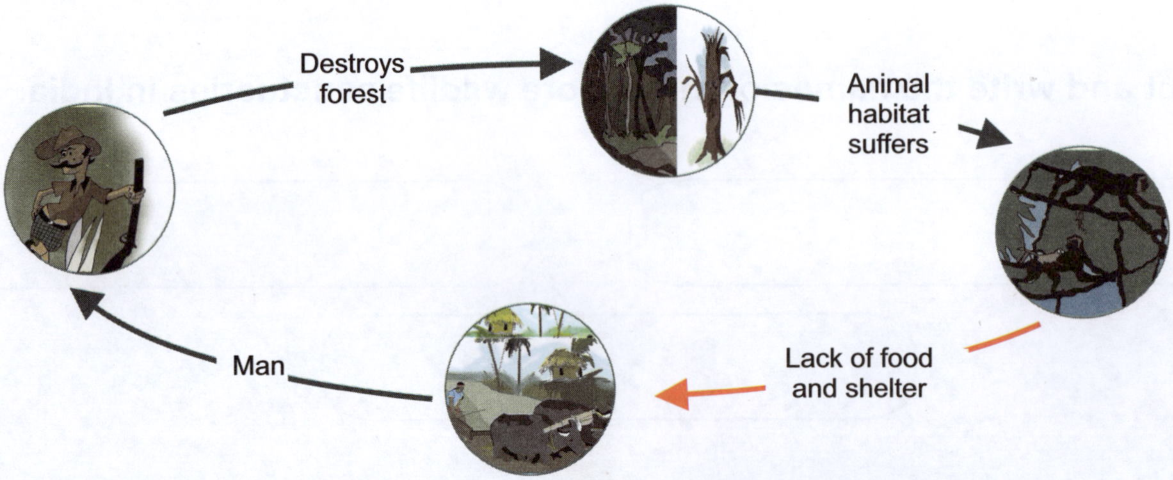

Fascinating Facts

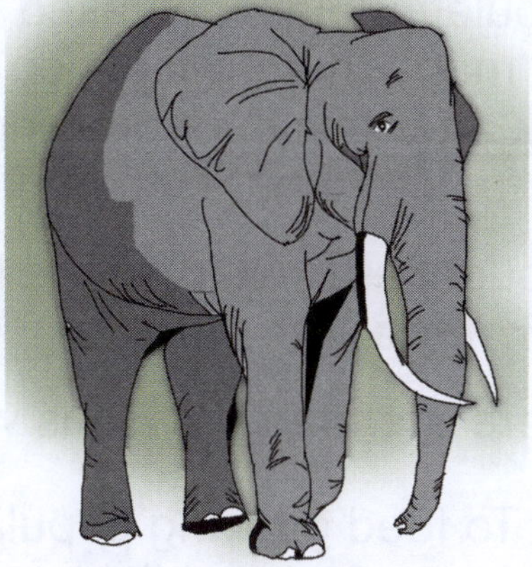

Elephants are the largest land animals. They sometimes weigh as much as 5900 kg and live up to 70 years. They drink about 180 litres of water and eat 150 kg of food every day.

Once upon a time, there were several species of elephants. Now, only the Asian and African species survive. Most of them live in wildlife sanctuaries and national parks.

Think about it!!

It is said that an elephant never forgets anything. Do you think he will ever forget the cruelty that man has done to him?

Here is a list of some other animals that are also killed by man. This illegal killing is called **poaching.**

- Rhino is killed for its horns.
- Crocodiles are killed for their shiny, scaly skin.

Find out and write the names of three more animals that are killed for their body parts. ________________ ________________ ________________

Earlier, fur coats were considered very fashionable garments. A large number of animals like chinchilla, mink and even rabbits were killed for their furs. Now, fur is banned all over the world. People have realised their mistake. Fashionable people now wear fake fur coats instead of the real one.

Why Are The Forests Vanishing?

Population has increased tremendously and today, there are many more people on Earth than before. In order to look after this ever growing population trees are being cut faster than they can grow back.

Deforestation

Thoughtless cutting or felling of trees causes **deforestation.**

There are many reasons why trees are being cut.

- To feed growing population, large forests are cleared for agricultural fields so that crops can be grown.
- Trees are chopped down for firewood and to make furniture, paper, etc.
- Leaves and young shoots are eaten by domestic animals like goats and cows. This does not allow new trees to grow.
- For use in factories, for example matchbox factories.

Poacher

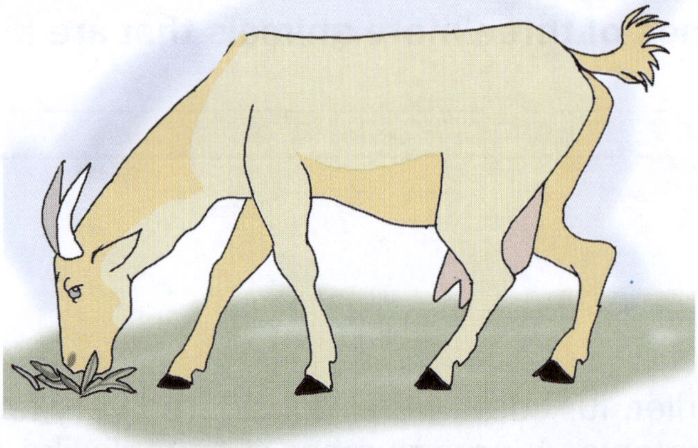

Goat eating newly born plants

When all these activities happen too often it leads to the destruction of forests. Forests disappear fast. New forests cannot grow so quickly. And, that is how deforestation takes place.

Sunderlal Bahuguna

But All Is Not Lost!!

Efforts to save forests and wild animals is taking place all over the world. Young people like you are joining in this mission.

Do You Know?

In 1973, the villagers, especially women in the Alaknanda Valley in Uttarakhand hugged trees in the forests, so that they could not be cut by the woodcutters who had been hired by the contractors. This care to be know as the CHIPKO movement. Its leader was Sunderlal Bahuguna.

Note To The Student

Find out one more state in India where a movement similar to the Chipko movement has been started.

How Can Forests And Wildlife Be Saved?

Following these simple steps will help you to contribute to wildlife protection. Here are some of them.

Chipko

1. When you go camping in the forests, do not leave garbage behind. Sometimes animals can get choked while trying to eat it.
2. Put out camp bonfires. Sometimes they can cause forest fires.
3. Do not break off branches of the trees.
4. Do not carve your names on the barks of the trees.
5. Do not take part in deliberate killing or hunting of animals just for fun.
6. Save paper! Avoiding wastage of paper will reduce the need to cut more trees.

The government has started relevant programmes like **Vanmahotsava** to protect the forests.

The government also likes to take the help of children like you to spread the message of wildlife protection.

The government is also taking the help of local people in protecting the wildlife of their area. They do so because local people have great knowledge about the place where they live.

You too can help save forests. Start a plantation drive in your school.

The government has also introduced the **Wildlife Protection Act** in the year **1972**. Under this act anyone caught killing wild animals, birds or plants will be severely punished.

Vanmahotsavas

Bookmarks can be made by students.
Posters and slogans on wildlife protection can be used to send out a powerful message.
Later, they can be displayed in the class a story.

Note To The Student

You can adopt an endangered animal and help it survive. Log on to : https://service.worldwildlife.org/opc

You will also be gifted a free T-shirt. Take the help of your computer teacher.

Survival Of The Fittest

Brontosaurus belonging to the Dinosaur family

When a very large number of a certain species of animals die and disappear from the earth, we say that the animal has become **extinct**. Sometimes animals are hunted to extinction, but interestingly there is another reason for animals becoming extinct.

Nature maintains its own balance. Sometimes there is a major change in the availability of food and climatic conditions and many animals are not able to adapt themselves to the changes in surroundings and die out. This is called **survival of the fittest**.

Millions of years ago the earth was inhabited by **dinosaurs**. But, after sometime they died. Perhaps, it was because they were not able to adapt themselves to the changes in the surroundings. When animals fail to adapt themselves to their natural surroundings they die and are lost forever.

Points to Remember

1. There are different kinds of animals found in the forests.
2. Most of the wild animals today live in protected zones called sanctuaries. The reason behind all this is that their natural habitats have been destroyed.
3. Poaching and deforestation by man are the two main causes.
4. Children can play an important role in protecting wildlife by following some simple practices.
5. When large numbers of a species of animal are killed, they disappear from the earth, we say that the animal has become extinct.
6. Government is also making efforts by introducing Wildlife Protection Act, 1972 and organising programmes like Vanmahotsava.

Think about it!!

It is said that wild animals like elephants and tigers attack villagers and kill people. They also destroy their homes and fields.

- Can we really blame them for such acts?
- Why are animals sometimes forced to leave the forest and go into the village?

Teacher to moderate discussion and encourage interaction.

Exercises

1. Answer the following questions.

(a) List out the reasons why animals need forests?

(b) What is deforestation?

(c) What is poaching?

(d) What are forests protected by the government called? Name some of them.

(e) List out the reasons why forests are vanishing?

(f) What was the reason behind holding the Chipko movement? Who was their leader and where did it begin?

(g) List out two things that you can do to save the forests.

2. Write short notes on the following.

(a) Project Tiger

(b) Wild Life Protection Act, 1972

(c) Survival of the fittest.

3. Write true or false.

	True	False
(a) Forests are home to domestic animals.		
(b) Animals are called nature's consumers.		
(c) Wild life sanctuaries are special homes for wild animals.		
(d) Man really does not respect nature.		
(e) Sometimes trees are cut to be used as firewood.		
(f) Carving names on barks of trees is a good habit.		

4. Match the following animals with the sanctuaries they are found in.

	Column A	Column B
(a)	Lion	Kaziranga
(b)	Elephants	Sunderbans
(c)	One-horned Rhino	Gir
(d)	Royal Bengal Tiger	Periyar

5. Write the years when the following events took place.

(a) Project Tiger ....

(b) Chipko Movement ....

(c) Wildlife Protection Act ....

6. Write four characteristics about elephants that you have read in the chapter.

7. Now write four characteristics about any one endangered species of your choice.

8. Find out what you know about tigers.

(a) They are found in .... National Parks.

(b) They are only .... in number left in India today.

(c) Project Tiger has been going on for .... years.

Fun Time

Conduct a mask making activity in the class where each student prepares a paper mask of an animal. Then, in front of the class speak a few lines about that animal.

Unit 3: Wildlife: An Important Natural Resource

Chapter 7

Forest Dwellers

Note To The Teacher

This lesson aims to help students understand the lives of forest dwellers. It is hoped that students will get to know about the difficult, but happy life of the tribals.

Learning Points

- Who are tribals?
- Which group is the oldest amongst the tribals?
- Main activities of the tribals.
- How deforestation is affecting the tribals?
- The tribes of Nagaland.

GLOSSARY

Natural vegetation, tribes, *adivasis*, datun, dams, protected areas, slash and burn method.

Hello Friends,

I am Barli. I am 12 years old. I live with my parents, grandfather and 5 brothers and sisters deep in the forests of **Chattisgarh.** Our village consists of about 36 families.

There are many children like me. We all play in the forests and have a lot of fun. We do not have much contact with the people outside our village. That is because we live so far from all other villages and towns. There are no proper roads for us to travel to cities and towns.

The elders in the village say that this is good for us because people from towns and cities only come and cut our forests and spoil the **natural vegetation.**

This saddens and harms all of us.

Children playing

Santhal

You must have understood by now that we are very different from other people.

We are **tribals, the forest dwellers**. We are also known as *adivasis.* Like most other tribes, we live in the forests. Our life is very different from others. I belong to the **Santhal tribe**. Many people of my tribe also live in other states like Bihar, West Bengal and Odisha.

What Are Tribes?

Tribes are groups of people who live in a special area, generally a thickly forested area. Tribes have their own customs and traditions. They also speak a language of their own.

Where Are Tribes Found?

Our country is called a **land of diversity** because people belonging to different groups live here in harmony. The oldest of them are the *adivasis* (forest dwellers). It is said that in our country there are about 68.7 million tribals living in more than 6000 villages in forests.

Tribes	Place where they live
1. Abhor	Rajasthan
2. Ahirs	Uttar Pradesh
3. Bagri	Rajasthan, Punjab, Haryana, Madhya Pradesh
4. Beda	Ladakh
5. Bhil	Madhya Pradesh, Gujarat, Rajasthan
6. Kolam	Andhra Pradesh

The largest tribal group in India are the **Gonds** who live in central India.

The **Bhils of Rajasthan** are the second largest. Bhils are hunters who use bows and arrows to hunt animals.

A Gond boy

How Do The Forest Dwellers Live?

We regard the wood in the forest as our own. Our lives are connected with the forests.

Bhils

We depend on forests for building our homes, providing fuel for cooking our food and, of course, for the fruits and flowers and some vegetables. Children love collecting the beautiful **mahua** flowers. We pick tamarind from trees to eat while playing. Before returning from play we pick jackfruits from trees, which are cooked for dinner.

Everyone in the village works very hard. **Farming** is the main activity. We grow small quantities of millet, maize, beans, etc. But, we also have some domestic and

poultry animals like cows and hens. We sell many forest products in the market to earn some extra money. These are some of the products that we sell- datun, firewood, dry fruits, bamboo, fish, timber, herbs.

We Need Schools

We, forest dwellers, are not very rich. We have a very difficult life. Everyone has to work and contribute.

Many people from my village have left and gone to find work in towns and cities. But, there is one big problem. As they have not attended school, they are uneducated and they can only get low paying jobs. Their chances of getting better jobs are very little.

One day some people from the government came to our village. A lady accompanied by three men came in a big jeep. They had a special meeting with the village elders. My grandfather also attended the meeting. They explained that the government wanted to open a school in the village for the children. "The key to development is education," they said.

Do You Know?

Datun is the green stem of the mahua tree or neem tree which is used as a toothbrush by many people.

The village elders explained that the children did not understand Hindi, so they could not study in Hindi language. Finally, it was decided that a primary school would be set up where we would study in our own mother tongue.

That night my grandfather explained to us that we must all go to school. The school timings and other activities would be adjusted with the harvesting, the so that during those times we could help our parents.

Madhab Bhaiya who is the only literate person in our village would now become our teacher. The government officials will soon build a small school with two classrooms for us.

Does your school also adjust its timings for you? What are your school timings?

____

____

Note To The Teacher

To discuss why adjustment of school timings is necessary in tribal areas?

Reducing Forests

We, forest dwellers, understand the value of trees. We know that we cannot survive without them. So, we do everything to protect them. We use trees only when we need them and only as much as we need. We do not waste anything of the forest. But, now things are changing.

Sometimes the government wants to build dams or roads. They send contractors and their team to the forests to cut the trees and make way to build these.

Sometimes we face another problem. The government declares our forest to be a protected area. And, since trees cannot be cut in protected forests, we are forced to shift to some other part of the forests. When this happens, we lose our land and the trees too.

What other causes do you think forces forest dwellers to leave the forest?

The first one has been done for you.

1. To make national parks and sanctuaries.
2. ____________________
3. ____________________

Note To The Teacher

To conduct this as a class discussion.

You have already learnt that unnecessary cutting of trees is called **deforestation.** Deforestation has resulted in loss of habitat for both animals and forest dwellers. We are also facing other hardships. My friend Jhabli and I have heard that in many places the river water is flooding the villages and killing people as a result of deforestation. We know that trees can reduce soil erosion by tightening the soil and not letting it get washed away during the rainy season.

So, we all want that new **forest laws** should be introduced where cutting of trees in forests is totally banned. That day will be a very special day for all of us. We have also heard of a lady called Medha Patkar who is trying to help tribals like us in Gujarat. This is what Madhab bhaiya told us about her.

Medha Patkar has dedicated her life to help forest dwellers and other villagers who are losing their lands and homes due to building of a very big dam called the **Sardar Sarovar Dam** on **River Narmada.** She has even gone on **fasts** several times to make sure the government provides all the help to the people. She has started a campaign called **Narmada Bachao Andolan**.

We Relax Too

You may be thinking that because of our difficult life we do not have time for some fun and relaxing activities. But dancing, singing and painting are very much a part of our tribal life. Regular fairs and festivals are organised where people from near and far come to attend. Special dances are performed. People come dressed in their best finery to attend such fairs. We love to wear jewellery. Some of the jewellery that we wear are **ear tops, garlands of flowers** and **coins, bangles, amulets,** and of course, we love to make new tattoos.

The World's Oldest Artists

Did you know that we tribals are the world's oldest painters and artists? Our themes have been the same for hundreds and thousands of years. We like to paint men, women, animals as well as God and Goddess. We also paint scenes of hunting, farming and festivity. We often do elaborate paintings during fairs and festivals. Almost all of us can paint but some of us paint extremely well. Earlier, vegetable dyes were used, but now acrylic colours are used too. We, generally, use wooden sticks as painting brushes.

Fascinating Facts

The earliest tribal paintings were found in **Bhimbhetka** and **Pachmarhi** in India. They are simple designs showing hunting, farming and dancing scenes.

The Thangkas are a tribal community residing in Ladakh. They follow Buddhism and make paintings of Lord Buddha on cloth.

We, forest dwellers, also use wood for carving beautiful designs. The most commonly made ones are beautiful birds and animals. By selling these wood carvings in the markets we not only earn some extra money, but are also able to show others how talented we are.

Do You Know?

90 km from **Vishakhapatnam** are a group of extremely old caves called the **Borra Caves**. The **River Gosthani** flows nearby. The entire region surrounding the caves is inhabited by tribals. They use it as a place of worship.

Have you observed how our paintings reflect our closeness to nature?

To The Land Of Shawl Weavers

Hello Friends!

I am **Ulupi.** I live many miles away from **Barli's** home in the northeastern state of **Nagaland.** Almost all people who live in Nagaland belong to different tribes. There are 16 tribes in Nagaland. Each has its own local language, dress and customs.

Do you see me in this photograph? I am wearing a colourful shawl dress with lots of jewellery. Our shawls may seem similar to your's, but actually each tribe weaves different colourful designs in their shawls.

Observe the two pictures below.

What differences have you observed. Note them down.

____

____

Shawl weaving is not the only handicraft we excel in. **Bamboo** is grown in plenty on our land and we make many items out of it. Mat, armchair, table, sofa, lamp shade and basket are just a few of them.

Do you, or your friend, have any items made of bamboo at your home. If yes, then do note them down here.

1. ____________________ **2.** ____________________

3. ____________________ **4.** ____________________

My brother plays the flute very well. He gives special performances during festivals. Flutes are also made of thin bamboo. They produce beautiful sounds with different tunes.

The cups we use for drinking are also made of bamboo and are called **chungas**. We welcome all our guests by offering them **rice beer** in chungas.

Though both Barli and Ulupi's traditions and culture seem to be very different, but they have one thing in common, they are very environment friendly.

Would you like to know more about the lives of Barli and Ulupi? Perhaps, you can find some books in the library on the life of tribals.

Fascinating Facts

Situated near Nagaland is the eastern most state of India called **Arunachal Pradesh**. A very well-known tribe of this state is **Tai-Khamti**. They practice farming by the **slash and burn method**. They use the farming land for a number of agricultural seasons and then abandon it for a long period of time. In this way, the fertility of the soil is retained.

Points to Remember

1. Tribals live in thickly forested areas.
2. There are thousands of tribal groups in India.
3. They grow crops and collect flowers and fruits from the forests.
4. Dancing, singing and painting are some common relaxing activities undertaken by the tribals.
5. Bamboo is used to make many big and small items.

Exercises

1. Answer the following questions.

(a) Who are forest dwellers or tribals? Name the largest tribe of the country.

(b) Prepare a table showing different tribes of India and the places where they are found.

(c) What do tribals depend on the forests for?

(d) What happens when forests are declared as protected areas?

(e) What is deforestation? What affect does it have?

(f) How is Medha Patkar helping people in forests and villages?

(g) How can the tribes in Nagaland be differentiated?

2. Fill in the blanks with the correct letters. (Hint:- These are the names of some tribes of India.)

(a) S _ _ T _ _ L

(b) B _ D _

(c) _ _ LAM

(d) A H _ R

(e) G _ _ D

(f) T _ I - K _ _ M _ I

3. **Match column A with column B.**

A	B
(a) Santhal tribe	Gonds
(b) Sardar Sarovar Dam	Borra Caves
(c) Largest tribal group	Chhattisgarh
(d) River Gosthana	Chungas
(e) Bamboo cups	River Narmada

4. **Below are some of things that the tribals use. Find out what they are called by them?**

(a) Bamboo cups ....

(b) Coins ....

(c) Datun ....

(d) Common dress worn by tribes in Nagaland ....

Fun Time

Divide the students in your class into equal groups. Choose a team leader who will bring a chart paper. All the team members should bring pictures of different tribal communities in India. Prepare a collage. Once ready, put up the collage in the class.

Chapter 8

Food Producers

Note To The Teacher

Who are farmers? Why do some farmers own a lot of land, while others own less land? Why are some farmers landless? Why are chemicals and fertilizers used for farming? Is there any other way to do farming? These are some important points that this lesson aims to explain to students. Teachers to sensitise students about the hardships faced by farmers.

Learning Points

- Improvement in irrigational facilities.
- Problems faced by farmers before building of dams.
- Differentiate between subsistence farmers and surplus farmers.
- Why are chemicals and fertilizers used by farmers?
- Who are seasonal and migrant farmers?

GLOSSARY

Farm machinery, chemicals, fertilizers, surplus farmers, subsistence farmers, godowns, irrigation, HYV seeds, seasonal migrant workers, Green Revolution.

Harkishan Singh is a **farmer** from **Punjab.** His village Sukhgaon is on the way to a very famous dam in India**,** the **Bhakra Nangal Dam**. Pandit Jawaharlal Nehru, the first prime minister of India, described this dam as 'New Temple of Resurgent India' (symbol of India's progress).

The village is about 38 km from the dam site. Many years ago before the dam was built, Sukhgaon and all the other neighbouring villages used to face a tough time. There used to be very little water for supplying to the fields. The farmers worked very hard, but the agricultural produce was very little. Harkishan's father had to depend heavily on the rains. He hoped that the rains would come at the right time. If it didn't, then the crops would die and life would become very hard indeed.

The whole family worked in the fields. Even the children in the family sometimes did not go to school in order to help their parents in the fields.

Yet, things were not so good.

And then, one day everything changed.

A huge big dam was built by the government. It was called the **Bhakra Nangal Dam** and was built on **River Satluj.** Suddenly**,** there was enough water in the fields. Tube wells were overflowing with water. The villagers were overjoyed.

The lives of the people of Sukhgaon had changed forever.

Read on what Harkishan has to say:

"By the time I grew up, our agricultural produce had increased by three times. I now keep the required portion of crops grown, for my family and sell the rest in the market and earn more money. With the money that is earned, I buy tractors and other farm machinery. I buy better quality seeds, fertilizers and chemicals to use in the fields.

The **Bhakra Nangal Dam** is a great boon to the villagers of Sukhgaon and to many other villages in Punjab."

A **dam** is a wall built across a river. It is generally made of cement and rocks. A dam stops the flow of a river. The water gets collected behind the dam and forms a lake. From there, the water is supplied to far off places where there is shortage of water through canals and tube wells.

Such a system of supplying water to crops far away from rivers is called **irrigation.**

A dam helps in:

- controlling the river water and reducing floods
- generating hydroelectricity
- providing water for irrigation
- saving a lot of money for the government.

Dams also have many disadvantages.

- Many villages get destroyed during construction of a dam.
- The path of the river changes leading to destruction of plant and animal habitat.
- Sometimes frequency of earthquakes increase due to dams.

Who Is A Farmer?

A person who lives in a village and grows crops on a piece of land is called a farmer. The life of a farmer is a very difficult one. A farmer devotes many hours of his life in growing crops. And then, he has to wait for many months to reap the benefits of his hard work.

How Does A Farmer Plan His Works?

1. A clear cut plan for the future is needed by the farmer. He should know which crop should be sown in which season.
2. How to buy good quality seeds and where to store them.

3. Which modern agricultural techniques will help in sowing of seeds and in harvesting.
4. When to provide sufficient water.
5. To carefully look after the crops as they grow.

Crops

How Did Farming Begin?

The first crops in the world were probably grown by accident. People noticed that spilled grain grew into a new plant if they got proper water and sunshine. Therefore, instead of going in search of food, they began to grow the crops in one place. That is how farming began.

Are All Farmers Similar?

No! India is a very large country. There are millions of farmers. Some are large land owning farmers, others have small areas of land. Farmers who own large areas of land are called **surplus farmers**. They produce more crops than they need. They sell the extra crops in the market which is popularly called **mandi**. Some farmers sell their extra crops to the government. Harkishan is also a surplus farmer.

Godown

What do you think the government does with the crops? The government stores the extra crops in big storage areas called **godowns.** When there is a shortage of food in some part of the country, then the government officers distribute this food to people in that area. The government also opens up ration shops in different parts of the country where goods are sold at cheaper rates.

There are other smaller farmers known as **subsistence farmers**. These farmers are only able to grow enough for themselves and their family. They do not produce extra to sell in the market.

They cannot grow more because of various reasons:

- less land
- less rainfall
- lack of dam, tube wells, canals and other irrigational facilities.

The Green Revolution

Let us read more about Harkishan's farm.

"An important change that took place in my state, some years ago, was the introduction of new kinds of seeds. The seeds were called the **High Yielding Variety or HYV seeds**. With the use of these seeds more crops could be grown on the same piece of land. In my fields, for example, I grow wheat and sugarcane. My agricultural production has increased tremendously.

It was a wonderful thing to happen and it came to be called the **Green Revolution.** The person who brought about these changes came to be called the **father of the green revolution.** He is **M.S.Swaminathan**.

However, there is one big problem. There are many small insects who eat the crops. So, I have to spray poisonous chemicals called **pesticides** on my crops. Though, these pesticides kill the insects, I have to be very careful because the poison present in the pesticides can end up in the food that people eat. It can make them very unwell.

Some insects and flies have developed resistance to pesticides, as a result pesticides cannot kill them. Hence, more pesticides have to be used. These insects cause a great deal of damage. The people in my village are worried about this.

The Panchayat members of my village had an emergency meeting last week to discuss this problem. We have decided to start growing some crops without using **chemicals fertilizers**. Two people from an **NGO** called **Suraksha** came to our village and told us how we could do this. We were told to follow a few simple steps:

- Use straw and rotting plants. They naturally enrich soil.
- Ploughing land so that air mixes with the soil.
- Remove unwanted plants which are known as weeds as they take away the important minerals from the soil.

I Cannot Go to School

Not everyone is as fortunate as Harkishan. There are many farmers in India who do not own large areas of land. In fact, they are not even subsistence farmers. Read the story of Vidyashree.

"I live with my parents and two younger brothers in a small village in Andhra Pradesh called Shrirangapuram.

Some years ago, my father owned a small area of land. It was less than 1 hectare in size, but we could still grow some rice which we all consumed. All of us helped father in farming.

Then, one day when I woke up in the morning I found my parents crying. They had been forced to give away our land as they had not repaid the money that they had borrowed from a rich farmer. We did not eat food that day. Soon, we all had to look for work elsewhere. My parents started working in the fields of the other farmers.

When there was no work in the village we would move to the city. We would all work in a construction site. My mother would feel very sad at times. But, my father says that one day we will buy our land back. I want to become a teacher when I grow up. But right now, I do not even go to school".

Farmers like Vidyashree's parents are **seasonal migrant farmers**. They do not have their own land. They work on the land of others. When their work is over they move to cities and return in the next season. Such farmers face severe hardships in their daily lives.

The Government Help

Our government is trying to help such farmers. Here is a list of steps the government is taking.

1. Giving money to farmers in the form of loans.
2. Providing free seeds and other fertilizers.
3. Providing better training to farmers.
4. Providing tube wells and equipment to farmers at low costs.

What else do you think the government can do?

Points to Remember

1. The Bhakra Nangal Dam is built on River Satluj in Punjab. It provides enough water to farmers in the form of irrigational facilities.
2. Some farmers produce a lot of agricultural crops. They are called surplus farmers.
3. Others produce just enough for themselves and their families. They are called subsistence farmers.
4. The building of dams and the introduction of Green Revolution has helped improve agricultural production.
5. Chemical pesticides and fertilizers are used by many farmers in their fields.
6. The farmers have to use pesticides and fertilizers very carefully as they can harm people and make them unwell too.

Exercises

1. Answer the following questions.

(a) Who is a farmer?

(b) Why is it said that the life of a farmer is a very difficult one?

(c) What steps does a farmer need to take to plan for the future?

(d) Differentiate between surplus farmers and subsistence farmers?

(e) What is a dam? What are the advantages and disadvantages of a dam?

(f) What are the advantages of using HYV seeds?

(g) What problems arise after using the HYV seeds?

(h) List some simple steps using which farmers can grow crops without using chemical fertilizers.

(i) Who are seasonal/migrant farmers? What hardships do they face?

(j) How is the government helping such farmers?

2. Unjumble the words in column A and then match them with column B.

Column A	Correct word	Column B
(a) ULSTAJ	____________	irrigation
(b) MSDA	____________	farm machinery
(c) ELWLSUBET	____________	big storage areas
(d) DWGOOSN	____________	Bhakra Nangal Dam
(e) ACTROTSR	____________	generating hydroelectricity

3. Who am I?

(a) I am a big dam made on River Satluj in Punjab.

....

(b) I am a farmer. I grow a lot of crops. I sell most of my crops in the market. What kind of farmer am I?

....

(c) I am a poisonous chemical. If sprayed too much on crops, I can harm whoever eats it.

....

(d) I am a farmer without land. I work on the land of others. Sometimes I work in towns.

....

Fun Time

Organise a visit to a nearby farm or the one in your hometown.

Find out

1. What crops are grown?

____

2. How many people work in the farm?

____

3. In what season are the crops sown?

____

4. When is the crop harvested?

____

5. Are pesticides and chemical fertilizers being used?

____

6. Does the farm produce surplus crops or subsistence crops?

____

7. Hold a small presentation in the class.

Chapter 9

Farming in the Mountains

Note To The Teacher

A case study of a village in Uttarakhand has been taken to make students understand how the life of villagers have changed in the past few years and its effect on all the inhabitants. Teachers should sensitise students about the hardships faced by villagers.

Learning Points

- Natural beauty of Uttarakhand.
- Features of mountain soil.
- Subsistence agriculture.
- Solving the problem of shortage of water.
- Understanding terrace farming.
- Importance of community festivals.
- Changing times.

GLOSSARY

Himalayan mountain range, pilgrimage centre, mountain soil, subsistence agriculture, livestock, Uttarayani fair, cash crops.

Ram Dutt is a farmer. He is about 60 years old. He lives in **Itipur** village in Uttarakhand, which is a hill state in northern India. The hills are part of the **Himalayan mountain range**.

Uttarakhand is a land of great natural beauty. It has beautiful valleys, mountains and hill stations where tourists from all over the world come to rest and relax. Uttarakhand is a very popular pilgrimage centre as well.

Haridwar, Rishikesh, Badrinath, Kedarnath and Gomukh are some very popular pilgrimage centres. People from all over the world come to offer prayers and seek blessings from Gods.

1. **Can you name some well-known tourist spots in Uttarakhand?**

   ....

   ....

   ....

   ....

2. **Have you visited any of them?**

   ....

   ....

Uttarakhand is also a land of villages. There are big and small villages. Some are situated near the towns, while others are situated very high up in the mountains. Some villages are so remote that it is very difficult to even reach them.

Uttarakhand

Most houses have stone walls and thatch roofs. And, in the villages there are several farmers like Ram Dutt. For them, life is very harsh and tough.

The soil on which Ram Dutt does his farming is called **mountain soil.** Mountain soil is generally pale yellow or brown in colour. This soil is formed due to the breaking of mountain rocks, by rain, wind, ice and plant roots.

When Ram Dutt was young, farmers were dependent on rains for agricultures. The land was not very fertile. When it rained the crops grew well. There were very few facilities for irrigation. Not more than a few crops could grow in a year. Animal and human waste were used as fertilizers. Some of the common crops grown included, pulse, wheat and rice.

Pulse

Wheat

Rice

The production of food grains was low. It was mainly **subsistence agriculture**. In other words, food grown was just enough for fulfilling the needs of the farmer and his family.

Ram Dutt used to combine working on the fields with maintaining livestock and collecting useful materials from the forests.In this way, he was able to earn enough to look after his family.

Note To The Teacher

Encourage students to read the previous chapter once again to understand subsistence agriculture.

Livestock meant that Ram Dutt had some domestic animals which provided him with dairy products which were consumed by the family.

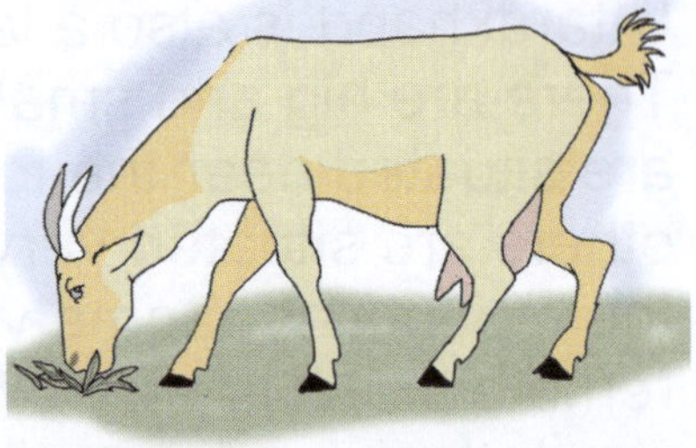

What animals do you think Ram Dutt may have domesticated? The first has been done for you.

1. Goats

2............................

3............................

Now, make a list of dairy products that Ram Dutt's family gets from his livestock.

1..............................

2..............................

3..............................

Harming The Environment

Overgrazing of meadows and forestlands and **cutting of wood** were the main reasons for deforestation. Ram Dutt and the others did not realise that the environment was also getting harmed.

Where Did The Water Come From?

However, Ram Dutt and the others realised that the shortage of water would be a big problem in the future. So, they built small **channels** for bringing the snow melted water from the mountains to their fields. Even with this improvement Ram Dutt could only manage seven months of **subsistence farming.**

Terrace farming

Terrace Farming

Just as in other hilly areas, the farmers of Itipur village practise **terrace farming**. Terrace farming means farmers build steps or terraces by flattening out an area, so that the water would not run off. The mountains in such a case look like a staircase.

Advantages Of Terrace Farming

Terrace farming is not only useful for farmers when they have no other land available, it also ensures good drainage of water and maximum use of irrigation water.

Community Festivals

Despite all the problems faced, Ram Dutt fondly remembers how the villagers still took out time for meeting their friends and relatives. And what better time for that than at festivals? How colourful everything and everybody looked. The whole village looked as if it was one big family.

The festival of **Basant Panchami** and **Makar Sankranti** marked the end of winters.

Basant Panchami

Makar Sankranti

Ram Dutt's favourite festival is **Phool Dei**. It comes in mid March and is celebrated to welcome spring. In the past, cooking used to be done in open fire using charcoal or wood. The heat from the fire cooked the food. So, the cooking was slow but the food was simply delicious.

Phool Dei

On the day of the Phool Dei festival, cooking would start early in the morning. The menu included gahat ki dal, raita, green vegetable curry, singal, kuleth phanu, with the desserts of Gulgula, Kesar Halwa and a very special pudding made of curd and jaggery.

Before the food was served to all, young girls would go from house to house in the village with a plate or thali of rice, coconut, jaggery, flowers and green leaves. The elders of each house would shower their blessings on them. Ram Dutt fondly remembers his daughters enjoying the festival in this manner.

Have you tasted gur? Find out the good qualities of gur.

Do You Know?

Jaggery is commonly known as gur in India.

The Times Have Changed

A lot of these are now only memories for Ram Dutt. The introduction of pesticides and chemical fertilizers changed agriculture forever. Farmers began to use more chemicals, pesticides and different varieties of seeds. This helped them grow more quantities of crops. But, this caused greater harm to the land.

The choice of crops also changed. Now, crops which could be sold in the market like wheat, maize, pumpkins, ginger, leafy vegetables and tobacco began to be grown. These crops were called **cash crops**. The farmers chose to sell more in the market, so that they could earn more money. Now they did not have time for meeting each other. Everyone was very busy.

Many more improvements were done. Electricity was brought in the village. A road was constructed, connecting the town to the village. Buses started driving up to the village from the town and back.

Tube wells now provided water to families. A health centre was set up and the doctor visited it twice a week. A school up to class 8 came up. And finally, television made its entry. There were movies, film songs, serials, news and children's programmes to watch. The means of recreation too began to change.

"We Don't Want To Stay Here"

Despite the improvements in the village, young people were leaving village to find work in the cities and towns. They felt that they would earn more money and have a more comfortable life in the towns and cities.

This migration of young people created an imbalance. It affected distribution of work.

In such situations, the work of young people now is performed by the old. All three sons of Ram Dutt have migrated from the village. The eldest Nitin is a soldier in the army. Second one Himanshu works as peon in a government office. And, the youngest Hemendra after being helped by his brothers in his education has become an IT professional in a private company. They have taken their wives with them to the city.

The fields and the livestock are being looked after by Ram Dutt and his wife now. They are worried about who will look after all the land once they are unable to do so due to old age. Ram Dutt's sons are already encouraging him to sell off the land and come and live with them in the city.

Ram Dutt cannot even imagine doing that. But in the depth of his heart he knows it is a losing battle.

Do You Agree?

Food For All

One evening when Ram Dutt was watching the world news on the TV, he was shocked to see young children belonging to another country looking weak, tired and sickly. The children were malnourished because there was severe shortage of food in their country. In other words, their country was suffering from a **famine.**

Famine occur because of heavy rains leading to floods which destroy crops and houses. Famine can also occur due to lack of rain or when no crops grow. This leads to **drought**. Sometimes, when a country fights a war with another country for a long period of time there can be shortage of food too. Without food, people become weak and fall sick. Many die of starvation.

Ram Dutt knew that in the olden days famines used to occur in India. He remembered his father telling him many years ago of a great famine in West Bengal.

Ram Dutt's father told him about the **Great Bengal famine** in the year 1943. At that time the land had dried up due to lack of rains. Thousands of people and animals had got affected.

Thankfully, Ram Dutt reminded himself, famines do not occur any longer in India.

Points to Remember

1. Uttarakhand is a land of great natural beauty.
2. The soil in Uttarakhand is not very fertile. It is called mountain soil.
3. In the past, the farmers could only do subsistence farming.
4. With the introduction of better farming techniques, farmers have begun to grow cash crops.
5. Young people are migrating from villages to the cities in the hope of getting good jobs.

Exercises

1. Answer the following questions.

(a) Describe the main physical features of Uttarakhand.

(b) Briefly explain the following.

- (i) Subsistence Agriculture
- (ii) Cash Crops
- (iii) Livestock
- (iv) Terrace farming
- (v) Famine

(c) List the various jobs that Ram Dutt undertook to earn more money.

(d) How has the village of Itipur changed from the olden days to the modern times?

(e) Why don't young people want to stay in villages any longer?

2. Mark True or False.

	True	False
(a) There are many tourist spots, but no pilgrimage centres in Uttarakhand.		
(b) Manduwa is a crop grown in Uttarakhand.		
(c) The Uttarayani fair is organised during the Phool Dei festival in Uttarakhand.		
(d) Famines occur sometimes due to heavy rains and sometimes due to lack of rains.		
(e) Wheat and maize are grown in Uttarakhand as cash crops.		

3. **Match the following.**

Column A	**Column B**
(a) Hill resort in Uttarakhand	Terrace farming
(b) Pale yellow or brown in colour	Rice, coconut and jaggery
(c) Severe shortage of food	Ranikhet
(d) Reduces soil erosion	Famine
(e) Phool Dei	Mountain soil

Fun Time

There are many changes that have taken place in the village of Itipur. Each bubble has one change written in it. Colour it with a crayon of your own choice.

Electricity

Shopping malls

Rail service

University

Health centre

T.V. network

Movie hall

School

Bus service

Unit 5: Shelter

Chapter 10

Different Places, Different Houses

Note To The Teacher

This lesson sheds light on the benefits of a house. It should be explained to the students that design and architecture of homes vary from place to place.

Learning Points

- A house gives us shelter.
- Houses are made according to the materials available in the area and the climate of the region.
- Houses are of different types.

GLOSSARY

Dwellings, stable, climate, pucca, kutcha, rangoli, dampen, traditional, modular, homeless.

We all need a house to live in. A house gives us shelter. It also protects us from heat, cold, rain and wild animals.

Can you think of any other thing that a house protects us from? A house is also a place where the family meets and talks.

What Is A House?

Any kind of dwelling where people stay is called a **house**. It can be a hut or a high-rise apartment.

Building material used for construction of houses are: Sand, clay, wood, rock etc.

History Of Houses

The earliest human beings did not have permanent dwellings. Many of them lived in dark caves when it was too cold and when the weather was warm they lived outside. They generally lived at the entrance of the cave to get some light and fresh air.

Times have changed, but even today houses are built to allow maximum light and air. Some places are hot throughout the year, while others are cold, some are dry, others are wet. Some get rainfall in the summer season, while others get it in the winters.

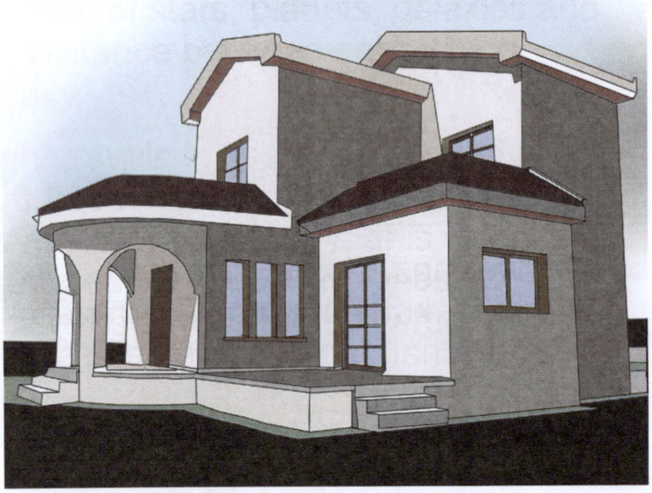

These changes in climate affect the design of houses.

There are some features that a good house should have. It should be:

1. strong enough to protect us against rough weather
2. located in green surroundings
3. airy, well lit and well ventilated
4. neat and clean and free from insects.

In cities and towns a house is made up of bricks, steel and cement. It is called a **pucca** or **permanent house.**

There are big homes and multi-storied buildings**.** These are called pucca houses. Sometimes houses are built with just bricks and the roof is covered with thatch and straw. Such houses are called **kutcha houses**. They are not as strong as **pucca** houses.

Do You Know?

Clay helps in keeping temperature stable.

Beating The Weather

Houses have to be built in a style that protects the people, who live in them, from the weather.

In hot countries, many houses have shutters to keep out the sun and keep the house cool.

In colder countries, houses have sloping roofs. Snow settles on the sloping roofs of mountain houses and helps to keep the heat inside.
In places that get flooded easily, many houses are built on stilts to keep them dry. They also have sloping roofs so that the water can slide down and not accumulate on it.

Homes of different Indian tribes have walls, which are decorated in pretty colours and painted with figures of birds and flowers. They are constructed without bricks, steel or cement.

Building Materials

Houses are made of different materials. In fact, different parts of a house can also be made of different materials. Let us read a little about them.

Walls

Walls are made up of different materials like bricks, mud or wood. The walls must be strong and dry. They have to be plastered with a mixture of lime, cement, sand and water to give them a smooth surface. Wooden walls have to be polished to give them protection and smoothness.

Do You Know?

5000 years ago people in India lived in houses made of bricks, wood and stone. They lived along the River Indus and were farmers.

With the help of your teacher, mark River Indus on a map of India.

High-rise apartments are common in the cities. Because of limited land and too many people, the buildings are often cramped together.

Types of Houses

- Terrace House
- Single House
- Apartment House

And also

Movable Houses

- House Boat
- Caravan
- Trailer House

Have you ever spent some time in a houseboat in Kashmir or in Kerala? Perhaps, you can talk about your trip in the class.

Different houses in India have different types of roofs.

Material used for making roofs are:

- straw
- asbestos sheets
- thatch
- stone
- tile
- palm leaves
- concrete

Fascinating Facts

In ancient Mesopotamia (modern day Iraq), about 5000 years ago, houses, palaces and shops were built with clay.

Note To The Teacher

Help students identify Iraq on a political map of the world.

Why Do We Need A Roof In A House?

A roof protects us from heat, cold, rain and thunder. That is why, a roof should be strong. It should not allow water to go through it and dampen the house.

Now let's see the different kinds of houses that are built in our country.

Sandstone is the ideal building material here. It is also very easily available. But nowadays cement is also used.

Some More Houses In India

In the Northeastern State of **Tripura**, houses are made of bamboo. These are called **Tang-ghar**.

In fact, bamboo is used for making almost everything here. Cane, thatch and timber are also used.

Traditional houses in Kerala are called **Nalukettu.**

When you visit Goa for your holiday, do not just have fun on the sea beach. Observe the traditional houses.

The houses in Goa are a perfect blend of **Indian** and portuguese style**.**

Movable Houses

Some people do not stay at a place for a very long period of time. They travel from place to place. So their houses also moves along with them. The number of people living in such houses is fewer than those in the traditional houses.

Mandap

Cattle herders like the **Gujjars** live in huts called **mandaps**. They are made of bamboo and grass.

You can see many such mandap settlements when you travel by road to Dehradun (capital of Uttarakhand). So plan a trip.

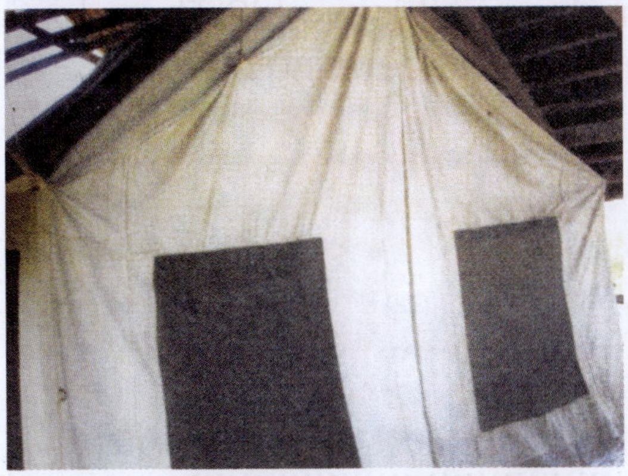

Tents

Nomads do not have a permanent place to stay. They travel from place to place and stay in tents which they wrap up when they move.

Who else do you think live in tents, even for a short period of time? Turn around the book to find the correct answer.

Answer : Soldiers

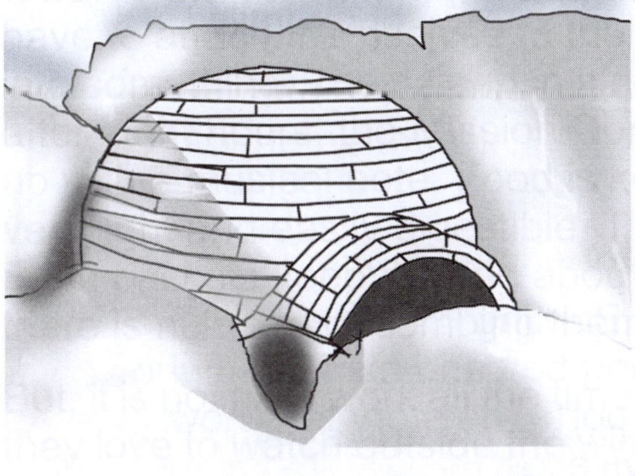

The **Inuits** from **Iceland** use ice to make their homes called **Igloos.**

Fascinating Facts

Laurie Baker was an **architect** from England who made India his home. He helped build very cheap houses for many people.

Modular Homes

Nowadays some homes are built in parts and then transported to the site of construction. Such homes are called **modular homes.**

They are as strong as regular homes.

Those Without Any Homes

But do you know, there are many people who are homeless in this world? They do not have any place to stay. You may have seen some of them spending a night under a bridge or the railway station.

What do you think happens to them when

It rains ....

....

It is a cold winter night...

....

Or a hot summer afternoon ....

....

Or when they are unwell ....

....

Activity

Read **Fly Away Home** By Eve Bunting.
It is the touching story of a young boy and his father who are homeless and live in an airport. The story tells how they find food and learn to survive.
It is a story filled with hope and determination. Take the help of your school library teacher.

Points to Remember

1. A home protects us from rain, heat and cold.
2. Houses are built of different materials depending on what is available and the climate of a place.
3. Houses should be comfortable places to live in.
4. Houses are very different in cities as compared to those in villages.

Exercises

1. Answer the following questions.

(a) How did early humans live?

(b) What are the features of a good house?

(c) How are pucca houses different from kutcha houses?

(d) How should walls be built in a house?

(e) Make a list of different types of houses.

(f) Name some materials used for making roofs. Why do houses need a roof?

(g) How are modern homes different from the homes of nomads?

2. Who am I?

(a) A dwelling where a family lives.

(b) A house made up of bricks and cement.

(c) A house with a sloping roof.

(d) A house from the ancient world of Mesopotamia.

3. **Match the following.**

Column A	**Column B**
(a) City	Caravans
(b) Mountain houses	Tribal Houses
(c) Decoration on walls	Pucca Houses
(d) Movable houses	Mandaps
(e) Cattle herder's home	Sloping roof

4. **Fill up the following blanks to get a clear picture of what houses are called in different parts of India.**

(a)	Kerala	N _ _ _ K _ _ T U
(b)	Tripura	T _ _ _ - _ _ _ R
(c)	Gujjar	_ A _ D _ P
(d)	Iceland	_ _ L _ _ S

Fun Time

What the teacher has to do — Share several property related advertisements with the students.

What the student has to do— After reading the advertisements, create an original advertisement about a house you want to put on sale.

Questions to put to yourself

1. What would you choose to emphasise in a limited space?
2. Which special features do you think the others would want to know about?

Later the advertisements can be placed in your class Notice Board.

Unit 5: Shelter

Chapter 11

Role Of Communities In Our Lives

Note To The Teacher

This chapter aims to explain to students, the importance of community living. It will help students understand that community living helps everyone to improve society.

Learning Points

- Definition of community.
- Importance of community life.
- Methods through which the community can be helped.
- How community can help children?

GLOSSARY

Community, inter-dependence, occupations, civic behaviour, environment.

We all belong to a large human group that lives in some part of the world.

But equally important are the many small groups that we belong to, like friends, neighbourhood, school mates, friends in your hobby classes or sports clubs.

These constitute our **community**.

An Ideal Community

Michael Collins from USA is an engineer by profession.

He has been living in India for the last one year. He chose to live in **Evershine Apartments**. What he did not know was that his neighbours had a heart of gold. In the middle of night, his daughter fell sick. She had severe stomach ache.
Mr. Collins did not know what to do? He contacted his neighbour and within minutes many other neighbours came forward to help him. Mr. Nagpal called up the hospital. Miss Radhika drove the family to the hospital. All the neighbours took turns to stay in the hospital when Mr. and Mrs. Collins went home to freshen up. The Collins family could not imagine that people in the apartments could be so nice. Mr. and Mrs. Collins were deeply touched by their kindness and thanked them.

All members of an **ideal community** help each other.

So What Is A Community?

To meet our needs we have to depend on each other. And in turn, we have certain duties towards others – our family, society and community.

You may be living in a colony or an apartment. The people living in your neighbourhood form a part of your community.

A **community** supports each other in times of joy and sorrow. Members of a community share many things and help each other in times of need. This means that we are always interdependent on each other.

Note To The Teacher

To discuss the concept of interdependence with students. There are many ways in which we can help our community. Helping our community is called **civic sense**.

Here are a few things that all the members of a community should do.

We can—

- Save electricity by making sure that the street lights of our colony are switched off early in the morning.
- Dump garbage only in dustbins.
- Stand in queues in our neighbourhood milk booth and vegetable shop.
- Park vehicles properly.
- Take care of young children and senior citizens.
- Participate in different social functions of all communities.
- Help neighbours in times of crisis.

Early Communities

Thousands of years ago, man lived in groups in caves. Then came villages and then towns and finally cities. The first known town was called **Catal Huynk** which is situated in modern **Turkey.** It comprised a community of people who were engaged in different jobs.

There are different type of people in a community. They may come from different parts of the world and might be engaged in different occupations.

List out some of the common occupations you can find within your community. The first one has been done for you.

1. Shopkeepers
2. ....
3. ....
4. ....
5. ....

Activity

In a community a postman is as important as a doctor. Interview some helpers in your community. You can follow the chart given below.

1. Name ______________________________
2. Occupation __________________________
3. How can you help to improve your community?

   ____

4. Do you think you are able to make a difference in people's lives?

   Yes____________ No ____________

Children Community Helpers

Children like you are the future global citizens. Helping the community will make you a better person.

A community can teach you many things. It can help you to:

- know more about society
- develop your talents and strengths
- understand others well
- share your joys and sorrows with others
- identify people who can support you for example doctors, police officers, lawyers, etc.
- learn about each other's cultures, religions and traditions.

Note To The Student

Have you ever thought how you can make your community strong? With your friends you can organise simple events such as a lunch get-togethers or run book clubs in your neighbourhood.

Organise a **'Neighbourhood Week'**. Each week encourage students to bring in photos of their neighbourhood, listing the neighbourhood buildings and events.

Now read this story. It will help you understand how even children can help a community.

Old Is Gold

"Papa, they began to cry when we sang old Hindi songs. One aunty took my hand and thought I was her daughter. She cried and I cried too", said Chitra to her father.

Eleven year old Chitra had visited an old age home with her school group and was narrating the details of the visit to her Father.

Many years later, Chitra grew up. She now studies in college. Her parents are confident that she will continue to help others.

They have taught her strong community values.

Environment-Friendly Community

Imagine your friend and you are walking down a hot and dusty road. And suddenly you turn in to a shady and cool lane, you heave a sigh of relief. There are innumerable trees lined up on both sides of the road.

Which street would you prefer to walk down?

Protection of environment is a very important part of our community life. All members of the community have to take up this responsibility.

You and your friends can do a lot to keep your neighbourhood green and clean.

Make a list of things you can do:

1. ....

2. ....

3. ....

4. ....

5. ....

Non-Governmental Organisation or NGO

NGOs play a very important role in community development. They help people who may be facing some problems. They help in building schools, hospitals, community centres, etc. They assist the government and the work they do benefits many people.

Other Communities

Rohan, who lives in Delhi, comes from Gujarat. During Dussehra festival, he and his parents go to the Central Park in the city where other people from Gujarat meet. They eat traditional food and have dance programmes for one and all. Most people are members of the **Gujarati Community.**

Rashi lives in England. On special occasions she and her family meet others in the temple or park. They are together known as members of the **Indian Community.**

Remember

For every tree that is cut, one more should be planted.

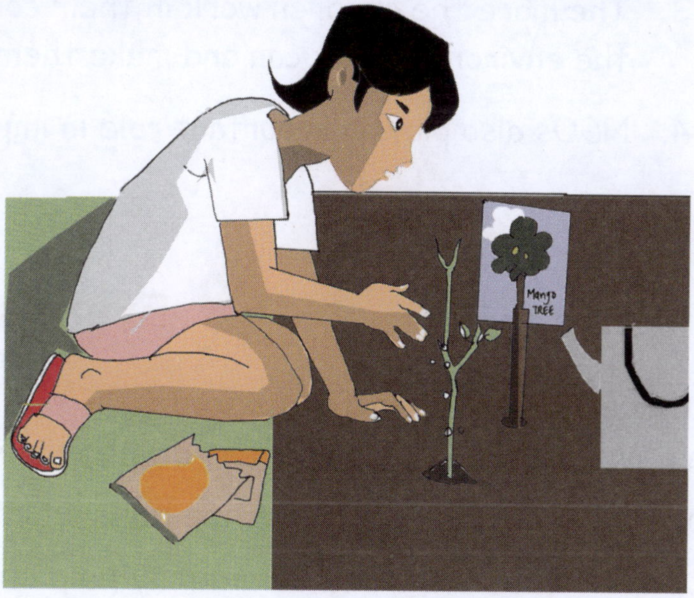

Additional Reading For Students

Read **Captain Snap and the Children of Vinegar Lane**.

This is the story of a group of children who care for an old sailor and learn the value of friendship.

Take help of your teachers and school librarian to find the book in the library.

Points to Remember

1. We need to live in a community for our own safety and security.
2. A community has people engaged in different occupations living in the same neighbourhood.
3. The more the children work in their community, the better they can make the environment. It can and make them selves more active and smart.
4. NGOs also play an important role in improving community life.

Exercises

1. Answer the following questions.

(a) What is a community? How do people in a community help each other?

(b) List some simple civic sense rules which all of us can follow?

(c) How does living in a community help children?

(d) What role do NGOs play in improving community life?

2. Put a tick (✓) mark on the correct column.

	True	False
(a) People living in our neighbourhood form part of the community.		
(b) Humans depend on each other.		
(c) Communities do not support each other in times of joys and sorrows.		
(d) In a community, people are engaged in different occupations.		
(e) The community is a window to the world.		
(f) Looking after trees is a very important part of community living.		

3. **Read this true story from Odisha "Meena girl".**

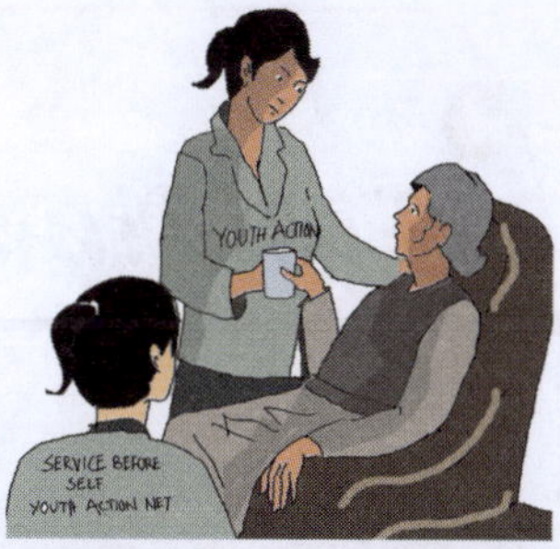

The United Nations agency UNICEF has made an animated film where the lead character is Meena. After the success of these short films in many states of India, **Meena didis** have come up.

They are young girls who are members of the **nature club** and lend help to local people. They help people in villages to study, keep the environment clean, and improve hygiene and public health. In other words, they help the community in all ways. Some of them have even won awards all over the world. One of them is Jyotirmayee Mohapatra. She has won the Youth Action Net Award.

In 1999, a terrible cyclone (hurricane) swept across coastal Odisha, the Meena girls joined hands with rescue teams and helped in every way they could. They also helped in distribution of relief material.

Aren't they important members of their community?

You can read in more detail about this story in http://www.unicef.org/india/child protection_475.htm

Now, answer the following.

(a) Who is Meena?

....

(b) Who are Meena didis?

....

(c) How has Jyotirmayee Mohapatra helped people of her community?

....

....

(d) Name some important people living in your community who have contributed to the benefit of your colony.
(Hint: They could be your or your friend's grandparents or parents too.)

....

Fun Time

Now do this activity to find out how much you know about the trees in your neighbourhood.

Find out the names of 10 trees near your home. Are they fruit bearing or flowering trees?

Name of tree	Fruit / flowering tree
....	....
....	....
....	....
....	....
....	....
....	....
....	....
....	....
....	....
....	....

Chapter 12

When Disaster Strikes

Note To The Teacher

This section aims to help teachers and students deal with common emergency situations. The chapter will serve as a training ground for helping students identify and give effective help during an emergency.

Learning Points

- What is disaster and emergency?
- Different types of disasters/emergencies.
- What to do in an emergency?
- How to provide First Aid?

GLOSSARY

Emergency/disaster, preparedness, earthquakes, floods, tsunami, first aid.

An **emergency** is a situation that constitutes immediate risk to life, property or environment.

An emergency could occur at any given moment of time. For example, you could be the first person to witness an accident. Your actions in these first few minutes when you provide immediate help to a person is very important.

Imagine yourself walking on the street. Right before your eyes you see a rider falling off his motorcycle and lying on the road unconscious and bleeding. What would you do?

Would you

- Run away and pretend you never saw the accident?
- Call for an ambulance?
- Find an adult and tell him/her what happened?

Road accidents, fires, floods, earthquakes, Tsunamis – you can encounter disaster anytime, anywhere. The most important thing is not to panic but to provide help.

In this chapter, we will discuss some common disasters and what to do when you are faced with one.

What Is Disaster?

A sudden accident or natural calamity that causes great damage or loss of life is called disaster. A disaster may affect a few people or a whole community living in an area. Disasters can lead to many injuries and even death. They require immediate action.

Remember

- You are never too young to help or to be trained for extending help.
- Preparedness is the key to facing any disaster.

At home, all family members should talk about

- Where to take shelter in a crisis?
- Where the first aid kit is kept?
- Prepare a list of people to be contacted during an emergency?
- How to turn off water and electricity mains when necessary?
- How to help a person with special needs at home or in the neighbourhood?

Note To The Teacher

Teachers can recommend the following websites to students. Here students will learn more about preparing for an emergency.
(a) http://www.whatstheplanstan.govt.nz/mcdem/index.htm
(b) http://www.pbs.org/newshour/infocus/floods.html

Disaster is of two types: **natural** and **manmade.**
Accidents due to human errors are known as **manmade disasters,** while **natural disasters** including earthquakes, Tsunamis, cyclones, etc. occur due to some changes in nature.

Earthquakes

Earthquakes are sudden and tremendous movements in the interior of the earth which lead to great vibrations on the surface.

Read this short story:

Munnia was lying in the bed fast asleep when a tremendous jerk woke her up. It felt like a gigantic hand was shaking her bed. The whole earth was trembling violently. Just then, her mother rushed in with her little brother. She pulled Munnia out of bed and shouted, "Run out. It's an earthquake!" Her father was racing ahead with their dog Moti. As they came out they saw their building come crashing down!

What Can You Do To Help?

Before the earthquake

- Hold earthquake drill, drop, cover and hold
- Prepare an emergency plan with adults at home or teachers at school.

During the earthquake

- Drop, cover and hold
- Stay where you are until the tremors stop
- Do not attempt to run outside

After the earthquake

- Follow all instructions from adults
- Stay calm
- Watch out for possible dangers or hazards
- Remember, there may be some aftershocks

Activity

On the political map of India mark the two areas where earthquakes caused major devastation, Bhuj in Gujarat and Tehri in Uttarakhand.

Animals have a sixth sense. It has been noticed that just before a disaster is about to strike, animals present in that area start showing strange behaviour. Dogs start howling and whining for no apparent reason.

Do You Know?

In **China** in 1975, just days before an earthquake, people had observed strange behaviour among the animals.

Note To The Teacher

Organise a workshop for children where they are provided training in Drop, Cover and Hold Drill.

Floods

Floods occur as a result of storms and heavy rains which cause rivers to overflow.
Here's a list of what you should do before and during floods.

Before the flood

- Find out the worst flooded area in the city with the help of your teacher.
- Keep valuables, food and water above the water mark.
- Move pets to safety.
- Keep chemicals and electrical goods in a safe place because if they leak, they can be dangerous.

During the flood

- Listen to weather updates on the T.V. and radio and other instructions carefully.
- Turn off electricity and water mains.

After the flood

- Only return home when it is safe.
- Do not go sightseeing through the flooded area.
- Drink water only after boiling. Contaminated water can cause severe stomach infection.
- Disinfect your house thoroughly.
- Wear rubber slippers, while using electrical appliances.

Name two regions in India where floods have occurred in the last one year.

1. ....

2. ....

Sonia's Story

Seventeen year old Sonia lived in a village in Tamil Nadu with her father, mother, elder brother, aunt and grandfather. On 26th Dec 2004, her mother, a fisherwoman, was on the beach when the water began to rise and gigantic waves began to form. The water flooded the land and swept a large number of people into the ocean.

Sonia struggled hard to help her brother who had a fractured leg, climb the roof of neighbour's house. As the water flooded the surrounding area and submerged her home. Forty-three people got swept away that day, including her mother, aunt, grandfather and father. Only her brother and Sonia survived.

Sonia was a courageous girl. She took up a course in Nursing, with UNICEF and now works with small children at the Aanganwadi centre. Sonia's mother always wanted her to be a nurse. She is now fulfilling her mother's dream.

Tsunami

Tsunami is a Japanese term made up of two words 'tsu' and 'nami' which means harbour wave.

Tsunamis are big waves that move in the oceans. They are caused by earthquakes or underwater volcanoes. During a storm, the high speed of wind causes the sea to rise and flood the land.

Tsunami can also occur due to the gravitational pull of the sun, moon and planets. It can also be caused by landslide or meteorite impact.

Mega Tsunamis are known as **Iniamis**. They can be worse than nuclear explosions in terms of death and destruction caused.

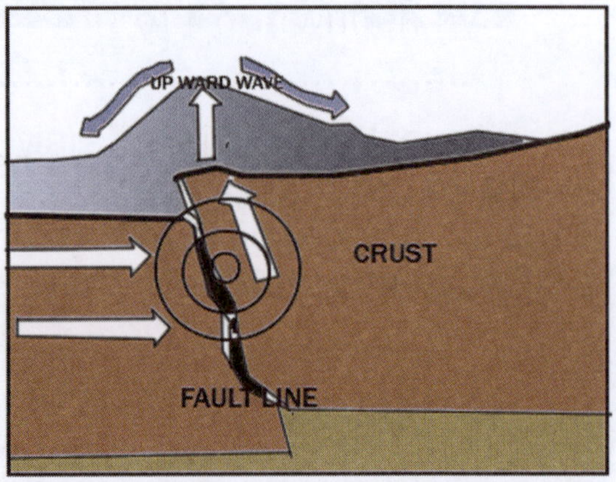

How To Help In An Emergency?

First Aid

Emergency can occur any time without warning. Therefore, everyone needs to be prepared so that victims can get immediate treatment. This instant treatment given to a victim is called **first aid**.

Fascinating Facts

Tribes from far off regions in the island of **Andamans** went deep into the forest just before the Tsunami-struck. How did they come to know of the impending danger? Think about it.

Remember, knowledge of first aid will give you confidence to deal with emergencies, no matter where you are.

You can learn first aid skills by attending a First-Aid Course in your own school. Take the help of your teacher.

First-Aid Course

The course will help you

- learn what to do at the time of an accident
- how to call for help
- how to deal with an injured person
- how to help someone who is choking.

Remember

ABC of First Aid. Check for

A- Airway - Check if the person is choking.

B- Breathing - Is the person breathing?

C- Circulation - Is there proper circulation of blood?

First Aid Kit

You can prepare your own **First-Aid kit**. But you should have the following tense:

You should have

1. a roll of cotton wool
2. a pair of small scissors
3. a roll of elastic bandage
4. a roll of cotton bandage
5. a bottle of antiseptic
6. some sticking plaster
7. safety pins
8. note book and pencil.

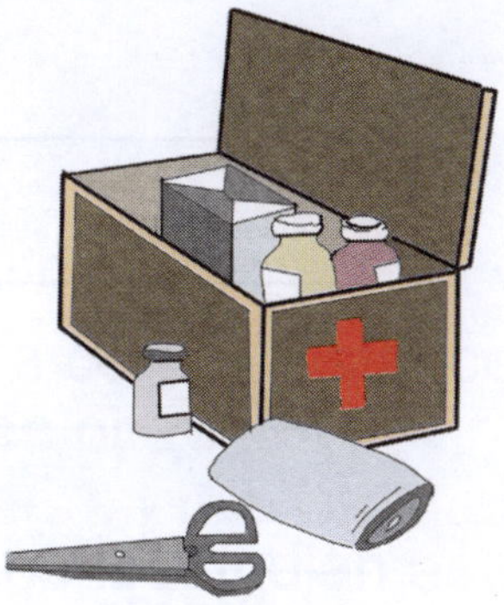

If you know even a little about what to do, it will be of great help.

Points to Remember

1. Disaster/emergency can strike anytime/anywhere. We have to be prepared for them.
2. Important natural emergencies are flood, earthquakes, Tsunamis, volcanoes, etc.
3. Manmade emergencies also exist like accidents, fires, etc.
4. All of us should have some knowledge of First Aid.

Exercises

1. Answer the following questions.

(a) What is an emergency?

(b) What is a disaster? How many types of disasters are there?

(c) How is an earthquake different from floods?

(d) What is a Tsunami? How are iniamis different from Tsunamis?

(e) What is First Aid? How can a first-aid course help us?

2. Now, make a diary containing all the important telephone numbers which may be needed in case of an emergency. Then paste them on your fridge for quick reference.

	Address	**Phone Number**
(a)	Police station	______________
(b)	Ambulance services	______________
(c)	Hospital	______________
(d)	Emergency	______________

3. **The following terms are jumbled up. to find what they are.**

(a) YCCONLES ……………………………….

(b) IMNTUSA ………………………………….

(c) SDOFLO …………………………………..

(d) THAERAQKUSE ………………………….

4. **Read the section on First Aid in the chapter again and then try to remember the things which should be part of your First-Aid kit. Now, write them in the chart below. Let's see how much you remember.**

Contents in the First-Aid kit	
______________	______________
______________	______________
______________	______________
______________	______________

5. **Put a tick (✓) for true or false.**

	True	False
(a) A sudden and great misfortune is a flood.		
(b) Preparedness is the key for facing any disaster.		
(c) During an earthquake you can save yourself with the drop, cover and hold technique.		
(d) During floods you should go sightseeing wherever you feel like.		
(e) During Tsunamis big waves in the oceans reach the land and destroy villages.		
(f) There should be a First-Aid kit in your home and school.		

6. Which of these medical problems, you think can happen due to floods. Shade the relevant bubbles in a colour of your choice.

Dehydration | Heart attack | Malaria

Fever | Diarrhoea | Tuberculosis (TB)

7. If there is an emergency at home, are you ready for it ? Tick (✓) on your answer.

(a) Do you have a First-Aid kit at home? Yes / No

(b) Do you know where it is kept? Yes / No

(c) Do you know whom to call if there is an emergency? Yes / No

(d) Do you know the telephone number of your family doctor, police and neighbour? Yes / No

Fun Time

Let's Discuss

Thousands of people lose their lives to road accidents every year. Yet, many accidents can be prevented by following some general safety rules.

Have a class discussion on what are some of these rules.

The first two are written for you. Add as many as you can.

1. Do not cross the yellow line dividing the road.
2. Use helmet if driving a two-wheeler or put on a seat belt if sitting in a car.

Unit 6: An Incredible Journey

Chapter 13

From The Mountains

Note To The Teacher

This lesson aims to introduce the mountain life to the students. The lesson highlights the hardships that mountaineers face and how they overcome it through sheer grit and determination.

Learning Points

- Definition of mountaineering.
- Equipments needed for climbing a mountain.
- Things to keep in mind while climbing a mountain.
- Problems faced by a mountaineer.
- Guidelines needed for a mountaineering expedition.
- Indian women mountaineers.

GLOSSARY

Mountaineer, athletic ability, equipments, expedition, avalanche, rappelling.

The children were waiting excitedly in the school auditorium. They knew that a well-known mountaineer would be coming to talk with them.

Mandeep Dhillon

The mountaineer gave an inspiring talk on what mountaineering was all about. He explained that mountaineering is a sport that could be taken up as a hobby or as a profession. It includes activities like hiking, trekking through valleys and climbing up mountains. It requires great athletic abilities and experience.

It also requires a lot of strength, determination, will power and desire to achieve the goal.

Physical strength is also greatly needed. The more physically fit one is, the easier the climb will be. The best exercise to become a mountaineer is to go walking or jogging. This helps in improving leg strength.

Some special equipments for climbing mountain are required.

In fact, climbing a mountain would not be possible without certain equipments and accessories:

- Woollen socks, jackets, sleeping bag and tent, windproof suits, goggles, trekking shoes and woollen caps.
- Safety harness, snow boots, ropes, helmet, Ice-axe, sunglasses, radio, emergency oxygen, cooking equipments and tinned food.

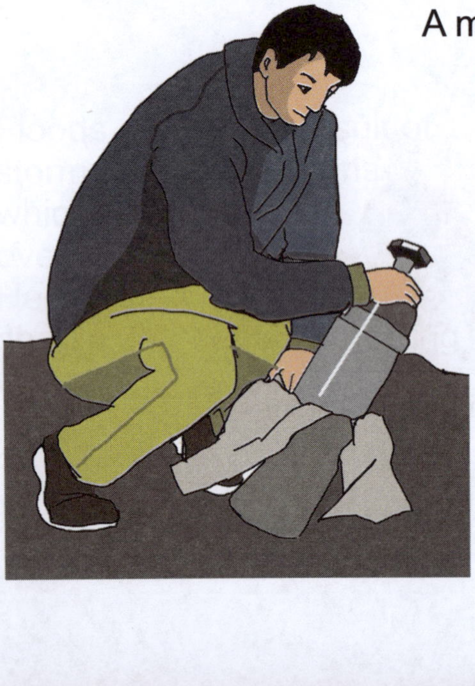

A mountaineer has to consider many things while climbing, such as altitude, weather, safety, health, food and water and terrain.

Altitude is the height of a place measured from sea bed. It is measured in feet or metres.

The weather high up in the mountains can change within minutes. It's sunny and bright one moment and the next moment icy winds can blow forcing every one to take shelter. So, preparing for any kind of weather condition and what shelter to take is extremely important.

Tents or Ice caves are the most common form of shelter used in the mountains. But, sometimes they too can collapse due to strong winds.

Note To The Student

Preparing for mountain climbing is similar to preparing your school bag for the day. If one book is forgotten, your work will suffer.

Another important decision that needs to be taken is where to set up the **base camp**. Base camp is the area from where an attempt to climb the summit of the mountain is made. Base camps have to be set up in such a place which is safe from rock falls or **avalanches**.

Hurdles

Despite taking care of many things, there are many problems which a mountaineer faces. Some of them arise from **falling rocks**. Rocks, which are constantly falling in the mountains are a major hurdle. Some days a few rocks might fall, while on others many more could fall. But, the danger is always there.

Sometimes climbing too fast in the mountains also leads to **mountain sickness.** Mountain sickness is caused by climbing up a mountain too high, too fast. As one goes up, the oxygen level decreases. When we give our body time to adjust to these changes, it is called **acclimatisation**. For example, when you climb 12,000 feet up a mountain, you have to stay there for few days to acclimatise.

There are also other discomforts which a mountaineer has to face:

- blisters on the feet
- loss of weight
- loss of sleep.

Motup: An Extraordinary Mountaineer

Motup was born in Kyagar village in the Nubra Valley of Ladakh situated in Kashmir. He climbed his first peak called Harmukh when he was just 13 years old.

His wife, **Yangdu Gombu**, is also a mountaineer. Her father, **Sherpa Nawang Gombu**, is the first man in the world to have climbed Mount Everest twice.

Motup

Do You Know?

Every mountain rock is slowly breaking up due to wind and rain.
When snow breaks loose and starts sliding down, it is called an **avalanche**. They are the biggest danger in the mountains.

Training Is Needed

Mountaineers cannot climb without proper training. Training includes almost everything. From

- choosing equipments
- tying a knot of the rope
- rapelling
- to finally planning the expedition.

The Nehru Institute of Mountaineering is the main institute where training is given to mountaineers. It is in Uttarkashi. It was established on 14th November 1965 to honour India's first Prime Minister, Jawaharlal Nehru, whose birthday also falls on that day.

Name the Indian teenager who became the youngest person to climb Mount Everest

____

Fascinating Facts

Mt. Everest is the world's highest peak. It is in Nepal. Its height is 8,848 m above sea level. It was first climbed on 29th May 1953 by Sir Edmund Hillary and Tenzing Norgay.

Guidelines Needed For An Expedition

Just as students follow some guidelines for completing their school work, mountaineers too have to follow certain important guidelines before the climb begins. They have to:

- check the level of their physical fitness
- undergo a medical test to make sure that they can climb for several hours at a stretch
- carry a set of important medicines
- undergo proper training
- make sure that proper protection is provided from snow blindness, frostbites and sunburn.

There are many well-known Indian women mountaineers. Bachendri Pal, Santosh Yadav, Dr. Harshwanti Bisht and Ricky Dolma are some of them. We Indians are extremely proud of them.

Bachendri Pal

Bachendri Pal was born in 1954 in the village of Nakuri in Garhwal, Uttarakhand. She started mountain climbing at the age of 12. It happened like this during a picnic with her friends she climbed a high mountain peak. Soon, it became dark and the friends had to spend the night at the peak without any food or shelter. That night she decided to become a mountaineer. When Bachendri grew up, she joined the Nehru Institute of Mountaineering.

She climbed Mt. Everest on 23rd May 1984 and reached the summit at 1:07 p.m. in the afternoon. After spending 43 minutes on the peak, Bachendri and her team returned to the awaiting applauds and cheers. Her guide was Brig.Gyan Singh from the Indian Army. She was later awarded the Arjuna Award and the Padma Shri by the government.

Bachendri Pal became a great motivation for many other women mountaineers, like Santosh Yadav who climbed Mt. Everest twice.
Santosh was born in 1969 and comes from the Rewari district of Haryana. She has also been awarded the Padma Shri in 2000.

Fascinating Facts

- Otzi was the first person ever known in the world to climb a mountain. He scaled a mountain 5,300 years ago in Europe. His body was fond preserved in a glacier by other mountaineers.
- The world's second highest peak is Mt. K2 in the Karakoram mountain range in the Himalayas. It is at a height of 8,611 m above sea level.
- The first woman in the world to climb Mt. Everest is Junko Tabei from Japan. She achieved this feat on 16th May 1975. Bachendri Pal is the 8th woman to climb Mt. Everest.
- Four women of the Indian Army Women Mountaineering Team scaled Mt. Everest on 7th August 2008.

Points to Remember

1. Mountaineering requires walking, trekking and climbing up mountains.
2. It requires possessing special equipments.
3. A mountaineer has to be prepared for many dangers and problems while climbing a mountain.
4. The world's highest peak is Mt. Everest at 8,848 metres above sea level.
5. There are many women mountaineers in India. They have all done India proud.

Exercises

1. Answer the following questions.

(a) What is mountaineering?

(b) Why is physical strength needed in mountaineering?

(c) What is the weather like high up in the mountains? What is the common form of shelter used by mountaineers?

(d) Write a few lines on

(i) falling rocks (ii) avalanche

(e) Name the highest peak in the world. What is its height? Who were the first mountaineers to conquer this peak?

(f) Make a list of the guidelines a mountaineer needs to follow while preparing for an expedition?

2. **Mark True or false by putting a tick (✓) on the correct box.**

	True	False
(a) To become a mountaineer a lot of determination is needed.		
(b) K2 peak is 8,613 m in height.		
(c) Santosh Yadav is the first Indian woman mountaineer to climb Mt. Everest.		
(d) Tents are the most common form of shelter used in mountains.		
(e) When snow breaks loose and starts sliding down, it is called altitude.		
(f) The Nehru Institute of Mountaineering is in Uttarkashi.		
(g) Bachendri Pal touched the summit at Mt. Everest on 22nd May 1994.		

3. **Who am I?**

Identify these famous mountaineers.

(a) I am known to be the first person in the world to climb a mountain.

(b) I climbed Mt. Everest along with Sir Edmund Hillary.

(c) My home town is in Rewari, Haryana. I have climbed Mt. Everest twice.

(d) I am the first person to climb Mt. Everest twice.

(e) The first peak I ever climbed was called Harmukh.

4. **Match column A with column B**

Column A	Column B
(a) How to tie a knot of the rope	8,848 m above sea level
(b) Mt. Everest	Area from which attempt to climb the mountain is made
(c) Ice - axe	Training
(d) Base Camp	Equipment needed for climbing a mountain

Fun Time

Mountaineering is a very good example of team work. Now divide yourselves into groups. Find information on Mt. Everest and name at least 10 Indians who have climbed it. Prepare a collage and give a presentation to the class.
Enjoy reading!

Log on to www.google.com and read the interesting story Hummel climbs Mt. Everest.

Chapter 14

Exploring The Universe

Note To The Teacher

The Universe is a detailed and vast subject. It is being introduced to students with this lesson. Teachers to give inputs wherever and whenever necessary. This lesson aims to reinforce, in young minds, the desire to achieve and also to instill a sense of pride for the achievements made by Indians in the space research.

Learning Points

- Definition of astronomy.
- What is a light year? What is a star?
- What is our home planet like?
- Who are astronomers? What is their main work?
- Famous Indian astronomers.

GLOSSARY

Astronomy, planets, galaxies, light year, astronomers, space detectives, telescope, spaceship, gravity.

"Can anyone tell me, how big is the universe?" asked Charu ma'am, our Astronomy Club teacher.

"The Universe is a vast space. It is bigger than the biggest of the continents on Earth and bigger than any planet or all planets put together", said Mariam, my best friend.

"Yes. And it is very, very old too. In fact, it is the oldest thing we know", said our teacher.

Charu Ma'am was conducting one of her astronomy sessions, which Mariam and I love to attend.

The desire to know about the Universe is not new. Even in ancient times, people used to observe the day and the night sky. Their study made them understand the Sun, Moon, Stars and the Planets and their effect on the Earth. From the movement of the heavenly bodies, they could predict the changing seasons. From their observations, they learnt to measure the time.

Astronomy is the study of all celestial objects such as planets, stars, galaxies and space.

Astronomy is full of numbers. The number of stars, planets, galaxies and the distance between each star or galaxy.

Light travels in space at a speed of 300,000 km per second. The distance travelled by light in a year is called a **light year**. It is used to measure distances across the universe.

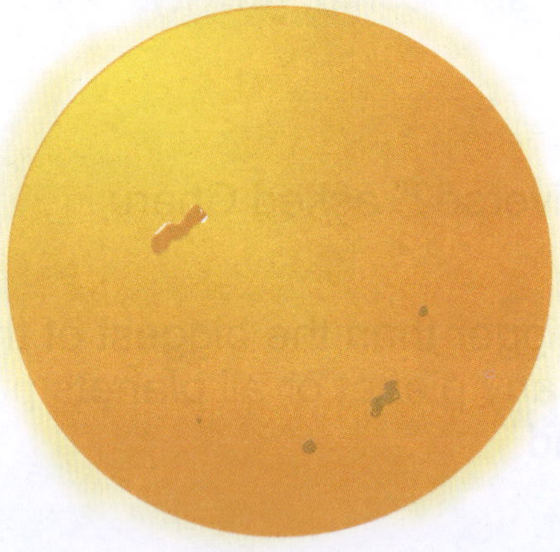

Sun

What is a Star

Stars are magnetic, spinning balls of hot glowing gases that shine throughout the Universe. The Sun is also a star. The **Sun** appears huge to us because it is closest to **Earth.** That's why the Sun outshines all the other stars.

Stars are extremely hot. They appear in different colours. The coldest stars are red in colour. Those stars which are very far from Earth look like twinkling dots in the sky. Those which are nearer to Earth look bigger. The brightest star is **Sirius**.

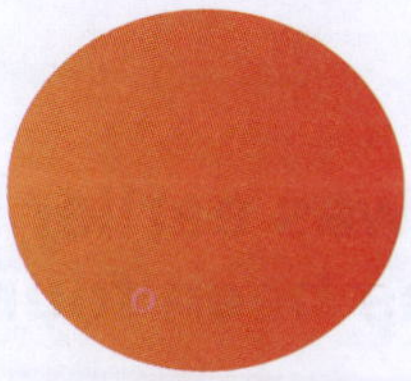

Sirius

The Planets

The ancient people looked at the star-like moving objects and called them **planets**, which means **wanderers**. The planets were named after the Roman Gods — **Jupiter**, king of the gods; **Mars**, the god of war; **Mercury**, the messenger of the gods; **Venus**, the god of love and beauty and **Saturn**, father of Jupiter and god of agriculture.

Home Planet

Planet **Earth** is our home. The Earth is an extraordinary ball of rock. It is 149.6 million km away from the Sun and revolves around it every 365.25 days at a speed of 30 km per second. Earth is the only planet known to have life.

Earth

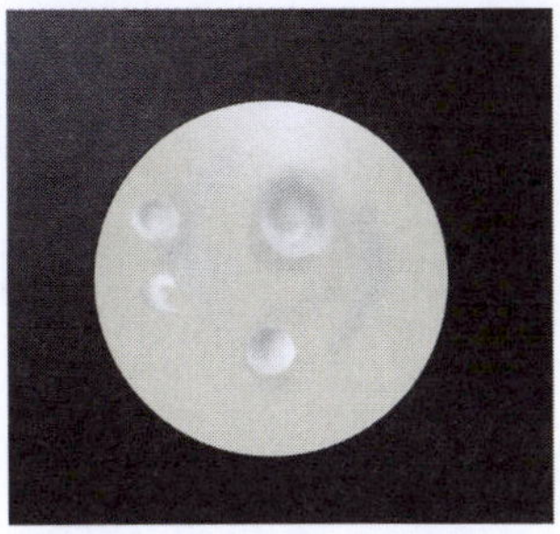

Moon

The Moon

Most planets have **satellites**. A satellite is an object moving around a larger object in space. It takes 28 days for it to travel once around the Earth. The moon's pull or gravity causes the Earth's oceans to rise and fall, which in turn causes tides.

It was earlier believed that other planets too had life on them. No proof has been found to substantiate that.

Exploring The Universe

In the next session, our teacher talked about the most interesting part of astronomy- Astronomers.

Astronomers are space explorers. They spend their lives finding out about stars and planets. They are also called **space detectives.** They find out about planets, stars and galaxies. They use powerful telescopes to peer into space and get information through telescopes, satellites and spaceships**,** sent from the Earth. And, sometimes they travel to space themselves.

Telescopes are optical instruments that are designed to make distant objects appear nearer.

Girl with telescope

Journey of A Lifetime

Travelling through space in order to visit and explore other world is called **space travel**. Over 400 men and women from all over the world have already travelled into space.

Do You Know?

The first living being to go to space was Laika, a dog from Russia.

Laika

Rakesh Sharma

The first Indian astronaut to go into space was **Rakesh Sharma**. Mrs. Indira Gandhi was the Prime Minister of India at that time. She had asked him how India looked from space. He replied, "*Saare Jahan Se Achha*" (better than the entire world).

Kalpana Chawla is the most well-known astronaut from India. She, along with seven other astronauts, travelled into space in a spaceship called **Columbia**. After completing all the research, the team was just 16 minutes away from Earth, when the spaceship burnt and disintegrated. Kalpana Chawla died, but her memory lives on and inspires millions of children all over India.

Kalpana Chawla

Sunita at treadmill

Astronaut **Sunita Williams'** father is of Indian origin. Though she has lived in the USA all her life, she loves India as her own country. She travelled into space on 9th December 2006.

Her **spaceship** was called **Discovery**. It travelled 360 km away from the Earth. Sunita Williams became the first person to run a marathon race in space.

Fascinating Facts

The first human being to go to space was Yuri Gagarin from Russia.

After returning from space, Sunita's life changed totally. She now watches less of T.V. and prefers to spend time with flowers and plants and go for long walks.

Sunita talking with children

Do you know what the Himalaya mountains looked like to her from space? "Like a wrinkle in a dress." And, the Earth looked like one big piece of land and water. Boundaries of different countries were not even visible. It was the most amazing sight for her.

On her visit to India, Sunita inspired children including those of her father's ancestral village, Jhulasar in Gujarat, with the following words.

"If you have determination, will and a dream, you can achieve what you want. You will face difficulties, but you will also learn to overcome them."

Life In A Spaceship

Sunita's diary records tell us a lot about life in a spaceship. Some of her recordings are as below:

- Astronauts decide their own menu which they will take to space.
- Water is retained and recycled. Nothing can be wasted.
- Living quarters are cramped.
- Vitamins and iron tablets are also taken by astronauts.

Astronauts relaxing

See How We Float

In a spaceship, there is no **gravity.** Gravity is the force by which all things move towards the centre of the earth. Astronauts become weightless. While sleeping they have to attach themselves to their beds, so that they do not float around or bump into something. They sleep in sleeping bags. When it is time to wake up, generally after eight hours, the Mission Control at NASA in Washington, DC, USA wakes them up with a musical note. Food is kept in special freeze-dried packets. Such meals are very light and easily digestible. They are a good source of energy and nutrients. Food packets keep floating about and long hair keep standing all the time. So, there is no need of combing them at all!

But, it is not hard work all the time. Astronauts too get some free time. During this time, they love to watch outside the window, specially the sunsets and the sunrises of earth which are very spectacular. They also watch movies, play cards, read books and speak to their families.

An Interactive Session

Before the astronomy club closed for the day, there was an interesting question-answer session. Here are some of the questions which were discussed.

Sunny : What would happen if the earth didn't have any gravity?

Charu ma'am : We would float away into space.

Priya : Why is space black and the sky blue?

Charu ma'am : About 20 km above the earth, the sky is black. Light travels in waves of different colours. Sunlight is a mix of all those different colours. The blue light gets scattered the most on earth. So, when we look at the sky during the daytime we see the scattered blue light.

Earth

Omar : Is our galaxy travelling through space or are we just spinning around the sun?

Charu ma'am : Yes, galaxy travels through space while we are spinning around the sun.

In Remembrance

Before the children left, Mariam and I got up. We told our teacher that we had come across a poem written by Kalpana Chawla to her friend on the internet. And, we wanted to recite it in the class.

Here is the poem by Kalpana:

Dive deep down,
an aim awaits.
Pearls peep,
for your hands to reach,
Just yours.
for years, decades and ages,
a door lies locked,
a pearl in the shell,
a secret in the brain,
open it, break it, reveal it, fly high.

Kalpana Chawla (27th October 1980)

Yes, Kalpana, we the children of India will fly high!

Points to Remember

1. The Universe is a vast space and is very, very old.
2. The study of the universe is called astronomy.
3. Distance travelled by light in a year is called light year.
4. Stars are huge spinning balls.
5. Earth is the only planet with life on it.
6. People who travel in space are called astronauts.
7. Rakesh Sharma, Kalpana Chawla and Sunita Williams are astronauts who are of Indian origin.

Exercises

1. Answer the following questions.

(a) Explain in brief
(i) light year (ii) universe (iii) star (iv) astronomers

(b) Write down some facts about Earth. Why is it so special?

(c) What happened to the spaceship 'Columbia'? Name the Indian astronaut travelling in it.

(d) How has astronaut Sunita William's life changed after returning from space?

(e) Based on what you have read in this chapter, make a list about how astronauts live in space.

2. Tell which of the following statements are true. Put a tick (✓) against the true statements. Correct the incorrect statements.

(a) In the olden days people could understand seasons by observing the sun, moon and stars.

....

(b) The study of rocks on earth is called astronomy.

....

(c) Gigantic, spinning balls of hot glowing gas that shine in the universe are planets.

....

(d) The brightest star in the night sky is Sirius.

....

(e) Astronomers are also called space doctors.

....

3. **Unjumble the following words.**

(a) PASCE = ____________ (b) AYXGLA = ____________

(b) ONOM = ____________ (d) AAKLI = ____________

Now read the sentences given below. Complete them using the unjumbled words from above.

(a) Earth's lifeless companion is the ....

(b) The first living being to go to space was a dog.

His name was ....

.

(c) Sunita Williams took this as part of her menu in

....

(d) Earth is part of it. It travels through space ....

4. **Neel has recently joined the Astronomy Club. He is a little confused. Can you help him find the correct answer? Tick (✓) correct ones.**

(a) I have forgotten the distance light travels per second. Is it **250,000 km** or **300,000 km**?

(b) Is **Earth** the only planet to have life. Or does **Mars** also have life on it?

(c) Are astronauts weightless in space or does their weight **increase, reduce** or **remain** the same?

(d) The sky is black above a certain distance from the earth. Is that distance **20 miles** or **20 km**?

(e) Was **Rakesh Sharma** the first Indian astronaut to go to space, or was it **Kalpana Chawla**?

Fun Time

You will require

A string with a ball tied at the end.

Imagine you are the Earth, the string is gravity and the ball is a spaceship.

Now start swinging the ball around in a circular motion.

You will see that the ball (spaceship) is pulling on you (earth) as you are pulling on the ball. (spaceship). If the string (gravity) was cut, the ball would fly off. Similarly, your spaceship will fly off in outer space.

The question is why does the ball (spaceship) not come to you (earth) as it swings.

This is because the ball (spaceship) is already in motion around you (earth).

This is like the spaceship. It is in motion around the earth and is continuously falling towards the earth (as the earth's gravity pulls on it), but since it is already moving around the earth, it is never pulled into the earth because it always misses it.

Interesting!!

Special note to students

Has this chapter motivated you enough to know more about astronomy? Do you want to learn how to build a spacecraft?

If so, then log on to **www.jpl.nasa.gov/scalemodels**

Or perhaps you would prefer to become an astronaut and fly in space.

Then log on to **edspace.nasa.gov/text/astroschool**

Chapter 15

A Visit To The Agra Fort

Note To The Teacher

This chapter is an introduction to history. With the help of a case study of the Agra Fort, students will be made to appreciate its historical importance and the reasons why the fort was built. Teachers to add inputs wherever necessary.

Learning Points

- Definition of a monument.
- Who were Mughals?
- Why are they called the Mughal dynasty?
- History of the Agra Fort.
- Building material used in the Agra Fort.
- Introduction of marble in Agra Fort.
- Layout and the gates of Agra Fort.
- Other important monuments in Agra.

GLOSSARY

Angoori petha, monuments, dynasty, Koh-i-noor, marble, drawbridges

Aastha was very excited. Her cousin Akanksha was coming to India from the USA for about two weeks.

Her mother told her that Akanksha didi was completing her PhD and was coming to India for further research.

After Akanksha arrived, she told Aastha that she was preparing a report on **Akbar the Great** and wanted to visit the **Agra Fort** built by him.

"Can I come along too?" asked Aastha.

"Yes, that can easily be managed. In fact, we all can go to Agra. Let me make the arrangements," decided Aastha's father.

Aastha clapped her hands in delight. It would turn out to be a very enjoyable trip. "And educational too," added Akanksha Didi.

Next morning the family started very early and by lunch time they had reached Agra.

Aastha's father had already got rooms booked at the government guest house. After they had freshened up they decided to visit the city of Agra. Aastha's mother wanted to buy shoes and embroidered suits. Akanksha wanted the famous **angoori petha.** These are some of the very well-known things in Agra. Is that all?

Agra is famous for its beautiful monuments and buildings, some of then are about 500 years old. And, it's these monuments and buildings that Aastha and her family are going to visit.

But first we must understand what a monument is.

A **monument** is a building or a structure specially built in honour of an event or a person. Monuments are generally found in places which are very old and have a long history.

The Visit Begins

Next morning after breakfast the family left for **Agra Fort**.

"The fort was built by the Mughals", commented her mother.

"Who were Mughals?" asked Aastha.

Akanksha explained that the **Mughals** were a very important family who ruled many parts of India for many generations. They introduced many important changes in India. Some of their family members are still living in this country.

Babur

When members of the same family rule for a very long period of time one after the other, it is called a **dynasty**. And, the Mughal dynasty is one of the longest ones to rule in India.

Some well-known **Mughal rulers** were Babur, Humayun, Akbar, Jahangir, Shahjahan and Bahadur Shah Zafar.

Let us join Aastha and her family in their discovery.

History of The Agra Fort

The **Agra Fort** has a very rich history. It was originally a brick structure that belonged to the Chauhan family. They were Rajputs.

Rajputs are people from Rajasthan, and are known to be strong, brave and heroic.

The rulers of the Lodhi dynasty made Agra their capital. It was then captured by the first Mughal ruler **Babur**. He defeated Ibrahim Lodhi in the Battle of Panipat in the year 1526. Babur found a vast treasure in the fort including the **Kohinoor diamond**.

Fascinating Facts

The **kohinoor** diamond is one of the largest diamonds in the world. It is now in England, The Queen of England wears it in her crown. The **Kohinoor** originally belonged to the ruler of **Gwalior** in **Madhya Pradesh**.

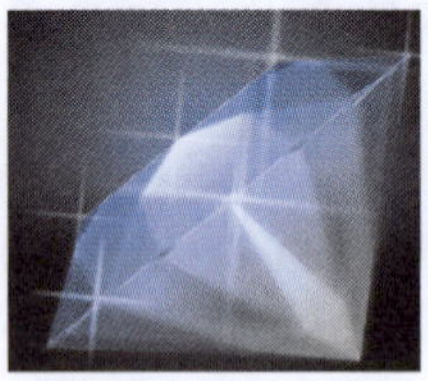

Babur's son Humanyun also ruled from the Agra Fort. When Akbar became the ruler, the fort was called **Badalgarh** and was in a ruined condition. Many parts of the building were in a dilapidated condition.
He rebuilt it with red sandstone. So it came to be known as **Lal Quila** or the **Red Fort** of Agra. 1,444,000 builders took eight years to complete it.

Remember

₹ 35 lakhs was spent on of Red Fort.
₹ 35 lakhs was an incredibly large amount of money in those days.

Note To The Teacher

To explain to students the value of ₹ 35 lakhs in that period.

Akbar got 500 buildings constructed inside the Agra Fort.

So, the fort was actually a complete city in itself. The design for making these forts was inspired from **Bengal** and **Gujarat**.

The walls had images of elephants, birds, dragons etc.

Unfortunately, today only 30 buildings structures are left other got destroyed in different wars.

The Introduction Of Marble

When Akbar's grandson Shahjahan came to the throne, he introduced some changes. He loved the use of **marble** and so he rebuilt some buildings inside the fort with marble.

Wall of the fort

Shahjahan built the famous **Taj Mahal,** one of the seven wonders of the world. It is called a **dream in marble**.

How Was The Agra Fort Planned?

Agra Fort is semi circular in shape. It is spread over 94 acres of land. **River Yamuna** flows on one side of the fort. The walls are 70 feet high.

In the olden day, wars between enemies were common. The walls of the Agra Fort were therefore built very high, so that the fort and the people living in it could be protected.

The walls used to have tiny holes from where the soldiers used to shoot arrows at their enemies. At the entrance of the fort mortar guns were kept. Sometimes hot water or hot oil used to be poured down on the enemy.

The **drawbridge** in the fort provided further security during war. Underneath the drawbridge water used to flow. And before a war, elephants were used to crush the drawbridge so that no one could enter the fort. Once the war was over new drawbridges were constructed.

Draw a drawbridge in your art file. Take your teacher's help.

Gates At Agra Fort

Aastha was not only amazed to see the fort but also to see the number of gates for entering the fort. Akanksha didi quickly drew a table to make it easy for Aastha to understand. You will also find it easy to understand when you read the following:

The Khizri Gate

This opens to the river Yamuna.

The Delhi Gate

It leads to an inner gate called **Hathi Pol** (the elephant's gate). Here two life-sized elephants and their riders are standing.

Khizri gate

The Lahore Gate

It is also called the **Amar Singh Gate.** All tourists enter from this gate.

The **Lahore Gate** was called so because it faced **Lahore**, which is now in **Pakistan** and the **Delhi Gate** facing **Delhi.**

Gates were very important in the olden days. They were huge in structure, so as to provide safety to the people inside the fort.

The engineers of that time had devised a unique, simple and effective system to save people from the summer heat. The walls were kept hollow and filled with running water so that the rooms remained cool. It was an amazing airconditioning system.

Khas mahal

On the way out, Aastha bought a small guide book to the **Agra Fort.**

She read some fascinating facts in it and she wants to share them with you.

1. The Agra Fort is bigger than the Red Fort in Delhi.
2. The Agra Fort has been mentioned in the Sherlock Holmes novel. **The Sign of Four** written by Sir Arthur Conan Doyle.
3. The great Maratha king **Chattrapati Shivaji** was cunningly captured by the Mughal emperor Aurangzeb and imprisoned here. But Shivaji heroically escaped.
4. A statue of Shivaji has been erected outside the fort in his honour.

Some of the sites and structures within the Agra Fort are:

1. Angoori Bagh, which has 85 square gardens.
2. Jahangiri Mahal, which was built by Akbar for his son Jahangir.
3. Mina Masjid, a tiny mosque. Tourists cannot visit it.
4. Sheesh Mahal a royal dressing room with tiny mirror-like decorations on the walls.

The Taj Mahal

There are two other well-known places in Agra—**Fatehpur Sikri** and **Taj Mahal.**

Akbar did not have a successor. It was after his visit to the famous saint of Agra, **Shaikh Salim Chisti,** that the king was blessed with three sons. As a gesture of thanks, **Akbar** built a whole new city in **Sikri.** But, it was soon deserted due to lack of good water system.

And finally the wonder of wonders — the **Taj Mahal.**

The **Taj Mahal** is one of the most famous buildings in the world. It was built by **Shahjahan** as a tomb for his wife **Mumtaz Mahal**.

It took 21 years to be completed and 20,000 workers and craftsmen worked to build it.

Mausamman Burj

Some of them came from Italy, Iran and Turkey. The Taj Mahal is 55 metres high and is made of white and yellow marble. Precious and semi-precious stones have been embedded into its walls.

Shahjahan's life ended in a very tragic manner. He was put in prison in the Agra Fort by his own son, Aurangzeb. He spent the rest of his life in Mausamman Burj, a tower with a marble balcony from where he could view the Taj Mahal. He never visited the Taj Mahal for the rest of his life.

Points to Remember

1. A building or structure built in honour of an event or a person, having a long history, is called a monument.
2. Families who rule for a very long period of time succeeding each other are called a dynasty.
3. The Agra Fort is over 500 years old.
4. The Mughal ruler Akbar rebuilt the fort with sandstone.
5. Shahjahan added marble designs to the fort.
6. Near to the Agra Fort are Fatehpur Sikri and the most beautiful monument in the world, the Taj Mahal.

Exercises

1. Answer the following questions.

(a) Explain in brief: (i) monument (ii) dynasty

(b) How did the Agra Fort come under the control of the Mughal Emperor Babur?

(c) How was the design of Agra Fort planned?

(d) How did the drawbridge protect the Agra Fort?

(e) Describe the gates in the Agra Fort. What was the need of having such large gates?

(f) What do you know about the Taj Mahal?

2. Fill in with appropriate words.

(a) The third ruler of the Mughal dynasty.

(b) The Agra Fort was originally with the family of these rulers.

(c) When Akbar became the ruler at the Agra Fort it was known by another name.

(d) This river flows alongside the Agra Fort.

(e) The name of the palace built by Akbar specially for his son Jahangir.

3. Match column A to column B

	Column A	**Column B**
(a)	Tower with marble balcony	Fatehpur Sikri
(b)	Taj Mahal	Elephant Gate
(c)	Agra Fort	Mausamman Burj
(d)	Shaikh Salim Chisti	Angoori Bagh
(e)	Hathi Pol	55 metres high

4. **Look at the painting below. Such paintings were very common and popular in the days of the Mughals. They were called miniature paintings as the size of the painting was small, sometimes surrounded by a wide border. The paintings were made involving great details and a large number of colours were used too. Each painting was very descriptive, i.e. it described a particular scene in detail.**

Observe the painting and answer the following.

What do you think this painting is trying to tell?

....

....

....

....

....

Mughal Miniature painting

Many people who visit monuments and old buildings do not understand the value of those buildings. They write their names and other things on the old walls. Some people even spit paan on them. Do you agree that what these people do is something totally wrong?

Perhaps, young children like you can make them understand the importance of our monuments and buildings.

Write a relevant slogan in support of saving monuments from being spoilt by people.

Later, all slogans can be put up in the class.

Look at the map of India.
Find out and colour the state which you belong to.

Political Map of India

World Political Map

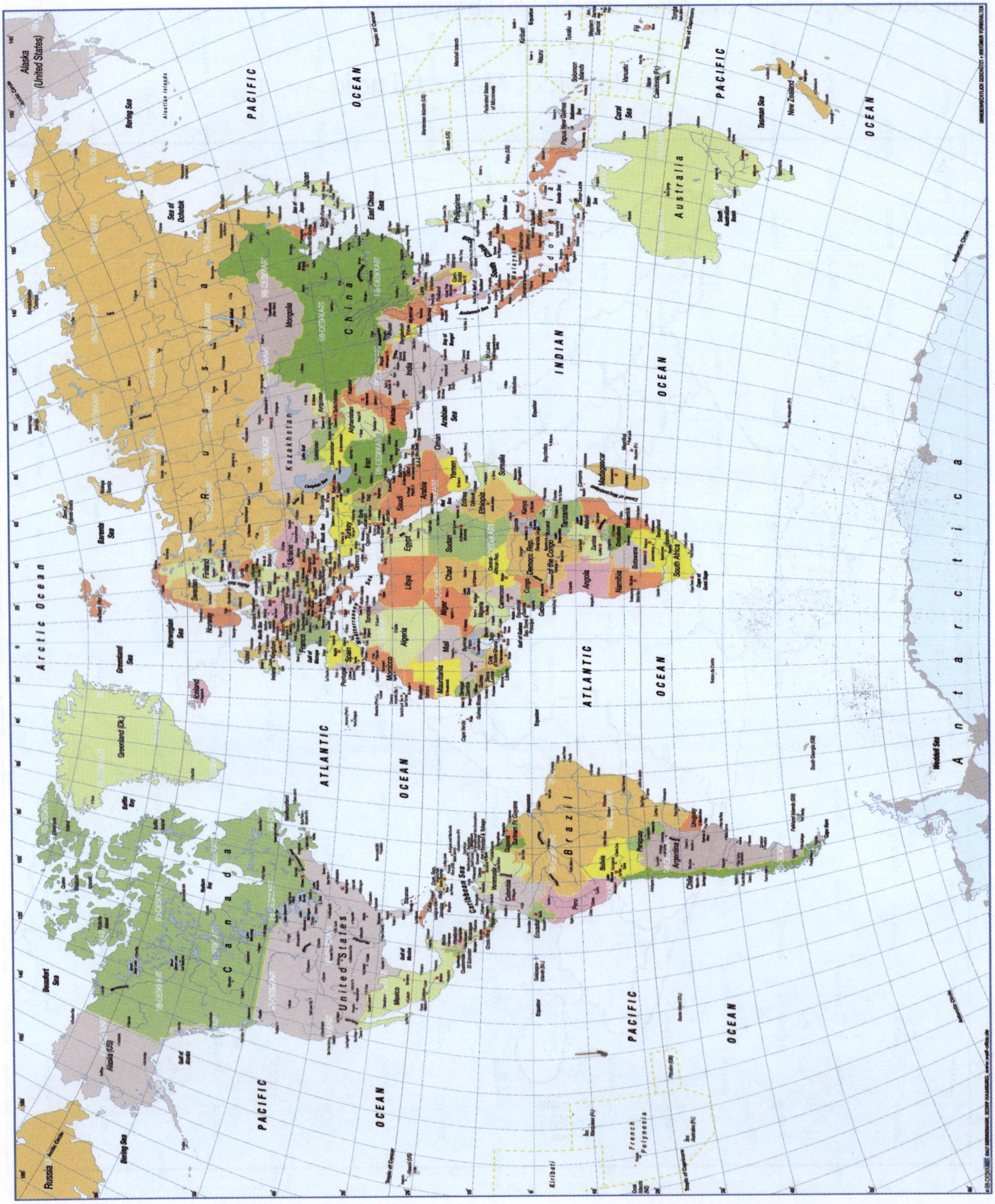